W9-CHP-958

A GUIDE TO HISTORICAL OUTINGS
IN SOUTHERN CALIFORNIA

Gloria Ricci Lothrop, Ph.D.

Historical Society of Southern California

Associated Historical Societies of Los Angeles County

Los Angeles: 1991

Copyright 1991
Gloria Ricci Lothrop

Library of Congress Catalog Card Number: 91-073513
ISBN: 0-914421-03-4

Cover design by Margaret Yasuda
Typeset by Christie Miles Bourdet
Printed in the United States of America
by Griffin Printing Co., Inc.
Glendale, California

A GUIDE TO HISTORICAL OUTINGS
IN SOUTHERN CALIFORNIA

Southern California Counties

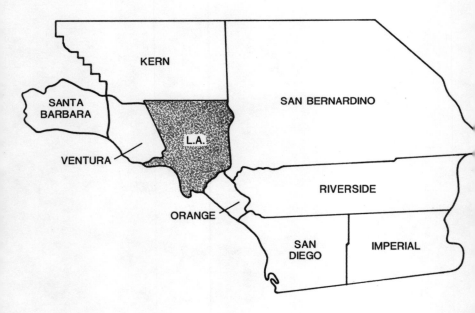

A GUIDE TO HISTORICAL OUTINGS
IN SOUTHERN CALIFORNIA

Map of Southern California Guidebook Area

Preface
Introduction
Acknowledgements

Map of Los Angeles County

The publication of this guidebook is made possible by a grant from the ARCO Foundation. The Historical Society of Southern California and the Associated Historical Societies of Los Angeles County wish to thank the ARCO Foundation and Mr. David E. Boyd, Director of Community Affairs, for this generous support.

Preface

History is alive and well in the Nineties! This is especially true of local history, perhaps the most attractive kind of history because more of us and our families are a part of it.

Local history is also the most immediate, personal and compelling kind of history. It is a history that speaks to the roots of where people live and from where they have come. It is a history that gives meaning and purpose and value to a community or a neighborhood. So it is understandable that interest in local history today should run at such a high level.

But so has frustration, because the resources for local history have not been identified, listed and explained in a way that the large number of history enthusiasts in Southern California can readily follow and fully utilize. What has been needed is an author with Dr. Gloria Lothrop's sense of place and history to produce this type of book, *A Guide To Historical Outings in Southern California.*

Therefore, the Historical Society of Southern California and the Associated Historical Societies of Los Angeles County are pleased to join forces to produce this important guide to the rich historical resources available in the Los Angeles/Southern California region.

We believe it is a guide that helps to take history out of the classroom into the community. It is a guide that enables individuals to *do* history, to be more conscious of themselves as historical beings and to be more aware of the power of history in their everyday lives. It is a guide that treats history as personal experience rather than as an abstract body of facts.

We hope it also is a guide that furthers cooperation and communication between historical organizations in Southern California, a guide that enables all of us to utilize to a greater extent the untapped potential we have in each other. And, if it continues to promote history as "the living past of the dead" rather than "the dead past of the living," our efforts will have been well served.

Thus we hope you will use this book as a planning guide to day trips and weekend outings for yourself, your family and your friends. With *Historical Outings* as your guide you can explore the many little-known corners of the southland, including those related to ethnic and women's history, architecture, business, sports, and the rich array of holiday observances.

Enjoy the high adventure that will come from this book!

Thomas F. Andrews, Ph.D., Executive Director
Historical Society of Southern California

Louis C. Bourdet, President
Associated Historical Societies of Los Angeles County

Introduction

This compilation of suggested trips to historic sites has been developed under the sponsorship of the Historical Society of Southern California and the Associated Historical Societies of Los Angeles County. It is intended as a planning aid for organizations, teachers of local history and individuals interested in exploring what remains of yesterdays built environment and material culture. The result of professional experience in organizing numerous college field trips and on-site workshops, it has been further enriched by a continuing personal interest in the many layers and the unexamined facets of the region's history. Where else would there be a museum containing a movie makeup artist's kissing machine, or museums devoted to the history of sports, music, banking, horse racing, printing, farming, auto racing, trains, planes and golf? Following the suggestions contained in this volume will lead to many others.

This guide began as a lengthy letter to a colleague responsible for historical society programs. The list of suggested outings grew to one hundred, then doubled, and soon tripled to become the collection presented in the following pages -- a representative, but not exaustive, guide to ways to celebrate the unexplored yesterdays of this uncommon region. While the City of Los Angeles, located on 451 square miles bounded by ocean and mountains, represents the largest area of any municipality in the world, the Los Angeles-San Bernardino Lowland represents a geologically complex, but relatively small geographic region. Capturing the ethos of this region is made even more complex by the fact that Los Angeles must be understood in the context of its fifty-five contiguous cities and suburbs, which at sunset spread out in a vast sea of illumination, which, Kevin Starr has observed, "in sheer extent is the horizontal equivalent of vertical New York."

The horizontal spread of settlement makes comprehensive walking tours problematic. It also has caused the emergence of many urban centers and an array of neighborhoods accessible but also made more impersonal by the automobile. The automobile which links Los

Angeles and has influenced its architecture, advertising, sociology and recreation patterns, is but one aspect of the technology that made possible what some have called the "self-invented city." Historic sites remind us of how Los Angeles, originally without water, harbor or economic hinterland, became a city in spite of itself -- a metropolitan region which today serves as headquarters to more than half the banking operations and industrial companies in the state, and whose port now handles 67% of California's international trade. Given the size of population, the variety of economic enterprises, and the consequent concentration of capital, it is not surprising the region, sometimes described as a "sixty-mile circle," extending from the bedroom suburbs of south Ventura County to north Orange County and inland to San Bernardino County, represents a gross economic product surpassed only by eleven political units in the world. Although this region occupies only 5% of California's land, its dense and varied economic activity, ranging from sportswear to aviation, from food processing to the manufacture of computer chips, represents intrinsic aspects of Los Angeles development awaiting exploration.

Further contributing to the rich complexity is an extraordinarily varied regional population surpassing twelve million. More scientists and engineers live here than in New York and Texas combined. The region is home to more Mexicans than anywhere except Mexico City. Quite appropriately, the region -- so strategically located on the Pacific Rim -- is home to the largest population of Koreans outside of Seoul, Korea. Here can be found more Japanese Americans than anywhere else in the world, more Samoans than in American Samoa, and more than ninety languages and dialects spoken in the schools. In recognition of the area's rich racial diversity, a multi-national array of ceremonies and celebrations have been included in this guide.

Although Los Angeles has been referred to as the nation's "new Ellis Island," the diversity of peoples is not recent. Before European settlement in 1769, it is estimated that the 5,000 to 10,000 Native American residents of the region included some New Mexico Pueblo Indians, Yaquis from northern Mexico, Paiutes and Utes among the residents of such local villages as Cahuenga, Topanga and

Cucamonga. When in 1781 Spain established El Pueblo de La Reina de Los Angeles, the eleven settler families, consisting of forty-four *pobladores*, included mestizos, twenty-six of whom claimed African blood. By the time an independent Mexico assumed control in 1822, local residents included Frenchmen, Hollanders, Englishmen and Italians. When in 1848, at the end of the Mexican War, the territory was ceded to the United States, and the diversity was further enhanced by pioneer settlers, disillusioned '49ers and Chinese rail workers. No wonder that speeches at the city's centennial celebration were delivered in three languages! Successive waves of Yankees, particularly in the 1880s, 1894-1914 and 1919-1925, and post-1945, further transformed Los Angeles, adding successive overlays of culture which often obscured earlier traditions. Thus Victorian homes supplanted earlier dwellings of adobe and tile and Micheltorena Street was wrongly thought to honor an Irishman, Michael Torrance, instead of a Mexican Governor of California. It is fortunate that a few examples of these eras and styles are extant, providing destinations which give material dimension to what otherwise would remain mere chronicle.

The foregoing factors could be used to define the patterns of change in the region over the past two centuries. Los Angeles has grown in response to a cycle of economic booms -- from cattle to land, citrus, oil, motion pictures, aviation -- which have successively and concurrently fueled the regional economy. The region was further shaped by the consequent waves of in-migration which recreated the southern California dream to reflect new values and expectations. Finally, to accommodate this continuing expansion, settlements were widely dispersed across the region in suburban strips laced together with interurban electric cars, buses and the ubiquitous automobile.

The variety and complexity resulting from the interaction of these three phenomena provide the themes for many of the proposed outings. They explore both the known and unknown corners of this community which has been described as a ". . . Zen order of overlapping probabilities, nets and clouds." Some outings have been organized by location within the "sixty-mile circle," but there are also trips to Santa Barbara, Kern, Imperial and

San Diego counties. Other sections of the book are organized around such topics as the arts, architecture, business, sports and frontier history and the histories of women and of Native Americans. There are also a number of suggestions for historical activities to mark holiday observances. Overall, the suggestions reflect a partiality for the little-known and a special delight in serendipitous combinations which will enhance the exploration and celebration of the roots and traditions of our regional history and culture.

The destinations and combinations are neither exhaustive nor definitive, but rather should serve as models for individual creativity and initiative in planning a personally interesting historical excursion.

Such a panoramic study is subject to certain limitations. While maps are included, we recommend the various county editions of the *Thomas Bros Maps Popular Street Atlas* and maps available from the Automobile Club of Southern California. The most vexing limitation, however, is the fact that information can soon be out of date. Telephone numbers and their area codes, and hours of access to sites, are subject to change. For this reason, and also because some sites allow access only by appointment, call before embarking upon an excursion.

Because personal schedules vary, in most cases we chose not to include names of individual speakers or tour guides. Suggestions for speakers can be provided by curators at historic sites, local historical societies and history departments at local colleges and universities. Be alert to news reports about local experts on historical subjects. Keep a file, pool information and consider developing a master list for program planning. Similar strategies would be useful in selecting bus companies and caterers.

In conclusion, not all historic sites have been included. Some of our selections may be closed or moved, and others will soon be opened to the public. New books and tours will become available to further enhance exploration of the historic environment. It is hoped such information will be shared with the author for inclusion in subsequent editions of this volume.

Acknowledgements

The author wishes to express appreciation to the Historical Society of Southern California and to the Associated Historical Societies of Los Angeles County for sponsoring this project. Particular thanks is offered to the Arco Foundation for funding the publication of the guide. Expressions of appreciation are extended to Pamela Bleich, Judson Grenier and Doyce B. Nunis, Jr. for their many useful suggestions made in the course of reviewing the manuscript. The very substantial assistance of Associated Editor Christie Miles Bourdet is particularly worthy of acknowledgement. Her knowledge of local history and her editorial skills made her essential to the success of this project. A very special vote of thanks is in order for the many volunteers from both sponsoring organizations who painstakingly verified each entry. Above all, each of us, compilers and readers alike, owes a great debt of gratitude to the many historical society members who have devoted themselves to the preservation and refurbishment of the historical resources which are the focus of the activities outlined on the ensuing pages.

August 1991

Gloria Ricci Lothrop
Pomona, California

Los Angeles County

I. AREA OUTINGS

Los Angeles County

A. Central:

It is the same old Los Angeles, only more beautiful. It has grown enormously in the years since I was here. Its shops are very fine; its new boulevards magnificent; its skyscrapers, scattered throughout the city, stand by themselves like great beautiful towers . . . . This remains one of the loveliest spots in the world.

Oswald Garrison Villard, "Los Angeles Kaleidoscope," *The Nation* (March 21, 1934).

1. Take a docent-led walking tour of El Pueblo Historic Park, including the restored Plaza Firehouse and the Merced Theatre, named by builder William Abbot for his wife Mercedes. Walk down Olvera Street, restored through the efforts of Christine Sterling in the 1930s, and see the exhibit on her achievements in the rear of the Avila Adobe. View restored rooms in the Sepulveda House, built by Eloisa Martinez de Sepulveda in 1887. Lunch at La Golondrina, housed in the Pelanconi House, the oldest brick building in the city.

In the afternoon take a guided tour of the Los Angeles City Archives, located in Piper Center, 555 Ramirez Street (213/485-3512). Or take a downtown walking tour (see Self-Guided Tours in Appendix A).

An added stop if time permits is the Los Angeles County Fire Department Museum, 1320 N. Eastern Avenue (213/720-5129).

2. At Casa de Adobe (4603 N. Figueroa; 213/221-2163) arrange a catered lunch made up of dishes which originated in Los Angeles: begin with Shirley Temple cocktails and offer Cobb Salad, Grapefruit Cake (all three created at the famed Brown Derby), Chili Size, Chiffon Cake, and Hot Fudge Sundaes (the latter invented at C.C. Brown's). The invited speaker could be a representative of a Southern California restaurant association.

1

3. Tour the Subway Terminal Building at 417 S. Hill and invite the Electric Railway Historical Association (P.O. Box 24315, Los Angeles, CA 90024-0315) to trace the history of the Big Red Cars. Lunch -- weekdays only -- at L.A.'s oldest restaurant (1908): Cole's P.E. Buffet in the Pacific Electric Terminal Building, 118 E. 6th Street (213/622-4090).

4. Take a docent-led tour of City Hall at 200 N. Spring Street (Las Angelinas: 213/485-4424). Arrange for a presentation on a history of Los Angeles politics in the tower reception hall, or attend a session of the Los Angeles City Council. Be sure to walk around the observation deck and pick out city landmarks with the aid of the mounted maps.

5. Visit the authentically restored 1889 Farmdale School on the campus of Wilson High School in El Sereno (2660 Fithian Avenue; 213/222-6659), where John Baur (CSU Northridge: 818/885-3566) could be invited to discuss his book *Growing Up with California*.

6. Following lunch at Salisbury Manor, 1190 W. Adams (213/749-1190) see:

North University Park, bounded by Jefferson & Vermont and 23rd & Figueroa, including *Queen Anne* houses at 2653 Hoover Street, 626 W. 30th Street, and 1007 W. 24th Street;

Bonnie Brae Street, the 800-1000 blocks, with fifteen homes in varied styles of the 1890s, *Queen Anne* predominating;

Chester Place, bounded by Adams & St. James and 23rd & Figueroa, including the 1901 Doheny mansion at 8 Chester Place (visit as guests of Mount St. Mary's College: 213/746-0450); and

the *Neo-Gothic/Romanesque* Stimson house at 2421 S. Figueroa, the St. Vincent de Paul Church at 621 W. Adams Boulevard and the 1300 block of Alvarado Terrace, stopping for tea at one of the several bed-and-breakfast inns.

7. Explore L.A.'s largest Christmas gift -- Griffith Park, including the 1830s Feliz Adobe at the Visitors Center, 4730 Crystal Springs Drive; invite the park staff to provide historical background (213/665-5188). The Center also has films and programs on varied aspects of nature study, and offers ranger-led nature walks. Ride the carrousel, and inquire about its history. Take box lunches aboard one of the antique trains in Travel Town at the north end of Zoo Drive (213/662-5874).

8. Tour the 1300 block of Carroll Avenue and Angelino Heights to view the lovingly-restored homes, mostly *Queen Anne* style of the 1880s. Take tea at the 1902 bed-&-breakfast Terrace Manor, 1353 Alvarado Terrace (213/381-1478), and inquire about the building's history; or sample a buffet at the Eastlake Inn, 1442 Kallam (213/250-1620), which specializes in theme repasts.

Arrange a visit to the 7,500-square-foot Victorian home which owners have converted into a private museum for a collection of organs, player pianos and other antiques (write: 1425 Miramar Street, Los Angeles, CA 90026).

9. Explore Bunker Hill "then" and "now" with a slide show of Leo Politi's paintings, followed by a walking tour of the area (714/629-2301). Enjoy box lunches in the Security Pacific Bank gardens, 333 S. Hope Street.

10. Invite a specialist on Witmer family history and archives to discuss the family's contributions to the early history of Los Angeles, at the Good Samaritan Hospital's Lucas Auditorium on the east side of Lucas Street (213/977-2555). For background information consult Virginia Linden Comer's *Los Angeles: A View from Crown Hill* and *The Witmers of Crown Hill.*

Note the nearby home of Mary Foy at 633 S. Witmer Street; the city's third librarian, she introduced L.A. to the Dewey decimal system. Lunch at the restored Mayfair Hotel, 1256 W. 7th Street at Witmer (213/484-9789).

11. Following lunch at Lawry's California Center, 370 W. Avenue 26 (213/224-6850), travel northeast on Figueroa along the Arroyo Seco. Recreate the world of Charles Fletcher Lummis with stops at his "El Alisal," 200 E. Avenue 43 (Historical Society of Southern California: 213/222-0546); the home and studio of Elmer and Miriam Wachtel, artists and founders of the Arroyo Arts and Crafts Guild, at 315 West Avenue 43; the Ebinger house at 369 N. Avenue 53; and several homes on Sycamore Terrace. Make special advance arrangements to visit the Judson Studios at 220 S. Avenue 66 (213/255-0131) and drive by the former bungalow home of Ernest and Alice Coleman Batchelder at 626 S. Arroyo in Pasadena. He was creator of noted decorative art tiles, and she organized the Coleman Music Concerts. Brochure and/or docent-guided walking tours are available through Highland Park Heritage Trust, P.O. Box 42894, Los Angeles, CA 90050-0894 (213/256-4326); or consult Gebhard & Winter, *Architecture in Los Angeles: A Compleat Guide*, pp. 341-359.

12. Arrange a visit to the Gilmore Adobe as guests of the A. F. Gilmore Company (P.O. Box 480314, Los Angeles, CA 90018; 213/939-1191). Tour adjoining Farmers Market at 3rd and Fairfax, and choose lunch from one of the many tempting food stalls. You may enjoy your meal upstairs in the Top-of-the-Market Gallery, where you might read aloud selections from Fred Beck's *Second Carrot from the End*, a lively story of the beginnings of the Farmers Market.

13. View the glories of West Adams Boulevard including Elegant Manor (3115 W. Adams), the 1909 Britt mansion (2141 W. Adams; 213/614-4111), and the homes of musician William Grant Still at 1262 Victoria Avenue and architect Paul Williams at 1690 Victoria, as guests of the West Adams Heritage Association (4311 Victoria Park Drive, Los Angeles, CA 90019; 213/935-6335, 737-7817). Lunch at The Cloisters, an 1896 Victorian home which has been transformed into a restaurant (2827 S. Hoover Street; 213/748-3528). Or, an elaborate dining experience is available to small parties at the nearby Maison Magnolia (2903 S. Hoover Street; 213/746-1314).

14. Relive the 1920s at Clifton's Silver Spoon, 515 W. 7th Street (213/485-1726), with a presentation by a California historian on the Townsend Plan, the Ham & Eggs Plan and the world of Clifford Clinton. View the second-floor exhibits on the history of Clifford Clinton's cafeterias and of Brock & Co. jewelers, former occupant of the property.

15. See "L.A. in the '20s" or "Turn-of-the-Century Los Angeles" in an all-day tour conducted by Round Town Tours; other tours of historical interest are also available

(310/836-7559). Tours are also available from The Next Stage (213/934-2216).

16. Explore the range of Glendale's history, beginning with the Casa Adobe de San Rafael, 1330 Dorothy Drive (818/956-2000). Then visit the 1888 Doctor's House in Brand Park, 1601 W. Mountain Street (818/242-7447). Also in the park is El Miradero which houses the Brand Library (818/956-2051).

Near Glendale, in the Eagle Rock area of Los Angeles, is Occidental College; "Oxy" campus tours are available (213/257-2700), and group luncheons may be arranged in Freeman Student Union patio (arrangements: 213/259-2737; catering: 213/259-2629). Take time to drive by the famed Eagle Rock, observable from Colorado Boulevard.

17. Tour Forest Lawn Memorial Park, 1712 S. Glendale Avenue in Glendale (Forest Lawn Community Affairs: 213/254-3131, 818/241-4151), viewing the various works of art and visiting its museum. Hear the remarkable story of Hubert Eaton, the creator of Forest Lawn. Having seen the setting, enjoy selected readings from Evelyn Waugh's novel *The Loved One*, or arrange for a showing of the old motion picture based on Waugh's story.

Notes

B. Hollywood and the
Entertainment Industry:

Hollywood . . . exists only as a state of mind, not as a geographical entity. One of the most famous place names in the world, Hollywood is neither a town nor a city, it is an integral part of Los Angeles. Despite its nebulous geographical status, however, Hollywood does exist as a community, but a community that must be defined in industrial rather than geographical terms.

Carey McWilliams, *Southern California: An Island on the Land* (1946).

18. Take a tour of early Hollywood, featuring films of the studios of Carl Laemmle and Thomas H. Ince, outtakes from the Cecil B. DeMille Studios and Mack Sennet's *The Ghosts of Hollywood*, made in 1931 -- presented at KCET's historic Little Theatre, 4401 Sunset Boulevard (213/667-9242).

19. Take a guided tour of the Hollywood Studio Museum located in the restored De Mille-Lasky Barn where the first feature-length movie, *The Squaw Man*, was shot in 1913 (2100 N. Highland Avenue; 213/874-2276). Visit the Hollywood Bowl Museum across the street at #2301 (213/850-2059).

Lunch at Musso & Frank's Grill, 6667 Hollywood Boulevard (213/467-7788). Spend the afternoon on the Grave Line Tour (310/392-5501) by chauffeured Cadillac hearse, visiting past celebrities in their cemeteries.

20. In KCET's Little Theatre (4401 Sunset Boulevard; 213/667-9242) view some early Hollywood classic films available on a rental basis. Invite a specialist in the history of film to comment; then take a guided tour of the KCET facility, for many years a motion picture studio, and note the plaque erected by the Los Angeles City Historical Society to mark the northwest corner of the original Pueblo de Los Angeles.

Make a day of it by taking a guided walking tour through a studio haunted by glamorous ghosts of Hollywood's past (Haunted Studios Tour, 6419 Hollywood Boulevard; 213/465-5224).

Your final stop will be to see the sunset from the Skyroom of the Yamashiro Restaurant, a stunning and authentic Japanese mountain palace with a real 600-year-old pagoda, reassembled in the Hollywood Hills in 1913-14 by Oriental art importers Adolph and Eugene Bernheimer (1999 N. Sycamore Avenue; 213/466-5126).

21. Tour the expanded facilities of the Margaret Herrick Library & Motion Picture Academy Archives, located in the artfully rehabilitated 1928 Beverly Hills Waterworks building, 333 S. La Cienega Boulevard, Beverly Hills (310/288-2220). Cinema memorabilia include scripts, photo stills and the first motion picture ever made, Thomas Edison's *Fred Ott's Sneeze*.

Follow with a visit to the Silent Movie Theatre, 611 N. Fairfax (213/653-2389).

22. Take the Hollywood Boulevard walking tour with Hollywood Heritage, and inquire about a visit to the restored El Capitan Theatre (Hollywood Heritage, P.O. Box 2586, Hollywood, CA 90028; 213/874-4005). Hollywood Boulevard received its name after Mary Penman Moll, Hollywood's first school teacher, circulated a petition to rename Prospect Avenue.

Lunch at the 1920s Hollywood Roosevelt Hotel (7000 Hollywood Boulevard; 213/466-7000), where the first Academy Awards ceremony was held; see the David Hockney swimming pool and the mezzanine-floor gallery of historical photographs. Also visit the miniature Hollywood created by cabinetmaker Joe Pelkofer on display at 6834 Hollywood Boulevard. Take the 6:00 p.m. tour with slide show describing the history of the recording industry at Capitol Records Tower, 1750 N. Vine Street (213/851-6135).

23. Join a two-hour tour of the Sunset Strip conducted by Hollywood Heritage (P.O. Box 2586, Hollywood, CA 90028; 213/874-4005). Lunch in the patio of Butterfield's Restaurant, the former home of John Barrymore (8426 Sunset; 213/656-3055).

Follow with a tour of the spacious Max Factor Beauty Museum with its several salons, photo and advertising displays; allow time to see the kissing machine, the personalized wig blocks and the several historic videos

(1666 N. Highland Avenue; 213/463-6668). A few blocks east is the Frederick's of Hollywood Museum of Lingerie (6608 Hollywood Boulevard; 213/466-8506).

24. Take a double-decker bus trip of Hollywood (Hollywood Fantasy Tours: 213/469-8184). Visit the camera collection of the Camera Collectors of America Society (213/876-5080) and the Hollywood Photographers Archives created by photographer Sid Avery (820 N. La Brea Avenue; 213/466-5404). Follow with dinner at El Cid Show Restaurant, in the first Hollywood sound stage, built in 1903 by D.W. Griffith (4212 W. Sunset Boulevard near Fountain; 213/668-0318).

25. See behind the TV screen in an NBC Studio Tour and visit the sound and special-effects center (3000 W. Alameda Avenue, Burbank; 818/840-3537); tickets to tapings may be requested. Or tour the home of Warner Bros. and independent production companies, 4000 Warner Boulevard, with live shooting included when possible (Warner Bros. VIP Tour 818/954-1744; sorry, no children under 10).

Follow with a visit to the Gordon R. Howard Museum -- with its collection of antique cars and cameras, exhibit on Warner Brothers' original *Jazz Singer*, Disney and NBC Studio exhibits -- as guests of the Burbank Historical Society (115 N. Lomita Street at Olive: 818/841-6333).

26. Join a two-hour tour of movie and television productions at Paramount Studios, 5555 Melrose Avenue, Los Angeles. Meet at the visitor center on the Gower Street side of the studio lot (213/468-5575).

Follow with a visit to the Hollywood Movie Costume Museum, 6630 Hollywood Boulevard (213/962-6992).

27. Participate in a Warner Bros. VIP Tour, which explores the studio facilities and includes live filming wherever possible (4000 Warner Boulevard, Burbank; 818/954-1744).

28. Take a guided tour of Columbia Pictures Studios in Culver City (310/280-8000). Follow with lunch at the Filmland Corporate Center (7000 Washington Boulevard, Culver City; 310/280-1700) featuring an invited speaker who will describe the Hollywood experiences of Faulkner, Fitzgerald and Dorothy Parker.

29. Watch live film and TV shootings with Hollywood on Location, which issues a list and map (8644 Wilshire Boulevard, Beverly Hills; 310/659-9165).

30. Relive the motion picture western with a visit to the Iverson Movie Location Ranch (P.O. Box 3096, Chatsworth, CA 91313; 818/700-9049).

31. Take a 90-minute ranger-led tour of a movie set of an old western town and attend an illustrated lecture on the history of Paramount Pictures at the Paramount Ranch in Agoura (818/888-3770). Take a picnic lunch, or have lunch at the Calabasas Inn, 2350 Park Sorrento, Calabasas (818/888-8870).

32. Visit the Roy Rogers-Dale Evans Museum, a 33,000-square-foot authentic replica of a frontier fort, filled with memorabilia and videos featuring some of the stars' earliest filmed appearances (15650 Seneca Road off Interstate 15, Victorville; 619/243-4547).

33. Take a walking tour of the Beachwood Canyon area of Hollywood with Neighborhood Place Project (8571-1/4 Rugby Drive, West Hollywood, CA 90069; 213/657-3733), including the 1924 hillside estate of Charles Toberman at 1847 Camino Palmero. Tour the 1907 Wattles Mansion and gardens at 1859 N. Curson Avenue, headquarters of Hollywood Heritage (213/874-4005).

Tour the Hollywood hilltop library of the American Film Institute, 5515 Western Avenue; 213/856-7600). Conclude at C.C. Brown's 1929 ice cream parlor (7007 Hollywood Boulevard; 213/462-9262), where the Hot Fudge Sundae was created.

34. Take a docent-led two-hour walk through the remains of the estate in Runyon Canyon once owned by Irish tenor John McCormack and later by Huntington Hartford (Friends of Runyon Canyon: 213/851-6135).

9

C. San Fernando Valley:

This day we set out about two in the afternoon, going north, as the explorers said that at the beach the mountains were steep and did not permit passage, so we veered somewhat to the northwest, where we saw that there was a pass in the mountains. We entered it by a canyon [Sepulveda] formed by steep hills on both sides, but at the end of it they were more accessible and permitted us to take the slope and ascend, though with difficulty to the top, whence we saw a very pleasant and spacious valley. The journey covered three leagues and we gave to this plain the name of Valley of Santa Catalina de Bononia de los Encinos [San Fernando Valley]. It has on its hills and in its valleys many live oaks and walnuts, though small.

From the diary of Father Juan Crespi, August 5, 1769.

35. Take a 90-minute tour of the Van Nuys Airport, the nation's busiest general aviation airport (818/840-8840). Continue the aviation theme with lunch at the 94th Aero Squadron Headquarters Restaurant (16320 Raymer, Van Nuys; 818/994-7437).

Arrange a visit to the historical museum at Los Angeles Valley College (5800 Fulton Avenue, Van Nuys; 818/781-1200 x373). Also view Judy Baca's portrayal of Los Angeles history, "The Great Wall of Los Angeles," extending 2435 feet along the Topanga Wash Drainage Canal on the east side of the campus.

36. Arrange with the Little Landers Historical Society to schedule a presentation on Southern California's utopian colonies at Bolton Hall, all that remains of the Little Landers community (10116 Commerce Avenue, Tujunga, CA 91042).

37. Visit the Merle Norman Classic Beauty Collection, which includes hundreds of rare mechanical instruments and classic automobiles (15180 Bledsoe Street, Sylmar; 818/367-2251).

38. Plan an outing to the Peter Strauss Ranch, where the lake and welcoming front porch of the stone ranch house invite picnickers (3000 Mulholland Highway, Agoura; 818/991-9231). An art show is held here annually in June.

Other possible destinations in the Santa Monica Mountains are the Diamond X Ranch (818/888-3770) and Wildacre Estate (818/769-2663).

39. Explore Los Encinos State Historic Park (16756 Moorpark Street in Encino; 818/784-4849), with its restored 1849 De la Osa Adobe and other American period buildings. Then tour the 1844 Leonis Adobe (23537 Calabasas Road in Calabasas; 818/712-0734), and the museum in the adjoining Plummer House. Lunch at Adam's (17500 Ventura Boulevard, Encino; 818/990-7427), and take time to look at the many historical photos on the walls.

On return through Mission Hills, visit the Andres Pico Adobe (10940 Sepulveda Boulevard; 818/365-7810), and take a docent-led tour of Mission San Fernando Rey de Espana, including a tour of the Diocesan Archives museum on the mission grounds (15151 San Fernando Mission Boulevard; 818/361-0186).

If there is time, visit the 1882 Casa de Lopez adobe (1100 Pico Street in San Fernando; 818/365-9990).

40. Tour the Orcutt Ranch Horticultural Center (Rancho Sombra de Los Robles) and Orcutt home, 23600 Roscoe Boulevard, Canoga Park (818/883-6641). Visit the museum of the Canoga-Owensmouth Historical Society, housed in a restored fire station (7248 Owensmouth Avenue, Canoga Park, CA 91303).

Also visit Shadow Ranch, part of the 60,000-acre wheat ranch owned by Isaac Lankershim and I.W. Van Nuys. It was purportedly here where the first stands of Australian gum trees were planted. Arrange for a presentation on the development of Southern California agriculture in the ranch house (22633 Vanowen Street, Canoga Park; 818/883-3637), now a community center.

41. In Newhall/Santa Clarita take the William S. Hart County Park self-guided tour of two-gun Bill's Horse Shoe Ranch house and a 30-minute guided tour of his larger home, Loma de Los Vientos, filled with memorabilia including five bronze sculptures by his friend Charles M.

Russell (24151 Newhall Avenue; 805/259-0855). Also nearby, visit the sites of California's first gold discovery and first oil refinery. See the Santa Clarita Valley Historical Society's Heritage Junction museums, the Saugus Train Station and Newhall Ranch House, at 24151 San Fernando Road (805/254-1275).

42. Visit Chatsworth Historical Society's Homestead Acre (10385 Shadow Oak Drive at the west end of Devonshire Street; 818/341-3053, 882-5614), for the annual Rose Festival on the first Sunday of May to see the famous rose garden at its best. Tour the Minnie Hall-Palmer Homestead Cottage, and visit the nearby 1903 Pioneer Church at 22601 Lassen Street.

See the exhibit and slide show at Santa Susanna Mountain Park Visitor Center, 22360 Devonshire Street, Chatsworth (818/884-9610).

Notes

D. Foothills & Pasadena:

As an indication of the character of this people, it is worthy of being recorded, that in the nine years of the history of the settlement not a single criminal prosecution has originated among its population of a thousand or more inhabitants, and only one civil case has been docketed by the resident Justice of the Peace in that time. Probably the same cannot be said of any other community of the same population in the State, or elsewhere.

A Southern California Paradise (In the Suburbs of Los Angeles) Being a Historic and Descriptive Account of Pasadena, San Gabriel, Sierra Madre, and La Canada; With Reference to Los Angeles and All Southern California (1883).

43. Arrange to tour the circa 1845 Adobe Flores (privately owned, write: 1804 Foothill Street, South Pasadena, CA. 91030). Visit the Meridian Iron Works building, headquarters of the South Pasadena Historical Society, at 913 Meridian Avenue.
Follow with a stop at the Castle Green Hotel, 99 S. Raymond Street (818/792-4444), and lunch at one of the many restaurants in Old Town Pasadena. After lunch, you may wish to browse in some of Old Town's antique shops.

44. Visit El Molino Viejo, the old mill of Mission San Gabriel, now the southern headquarters of the California Historical Society (1120 Old Mill Road, San Marino, CA 91109; 818/449-5450). Continue on to the Michael White Adobe, the oldest residence in the area, at 2701 Huntington Drive, San Marino; arrangements must be made through San Marino High School (818/568-0119). Proceed to the "Lucky" Baldwin estate, now the Los Angeles County Arboretum, 301 N. Baldwin Avenue, Arcadia (818/446-8251); tram tours of the extensive grounds are available.

45. Take a guided tour of Caltech's Jet Propulsion Lab, 4800 Oak Grove, Pasadena (818/354-4321). Arrange a visit to the privately owned, restored Hale Observatory in San Marino (818/793-559).
Visit the Mount Wilson Observatory as guests of the Mount Wilson Observatory Association (813 Santa Barbara

13

Street, Pasadena, CA 91101). Take Angeles Crest Highway north ten miles to Mt. Wilson Road (may be closed in winter; call ahead 818/793-3100).

46. As guests of the Ninth Judicial Circuit Historical Society, tour the historic Vista del Arroyo Hotel (125 S. Grand Avenue at Green, Pasadena), renovated to serve as headquarters for the U.S. Ninth Circuit Court of Appeal. Visit the three courtrooms, the Law Library, and the Little Mural Room featuring wall paintings by Terry Schoonhoven (Vista Docents: 818/790-0202).

Proceed to the former Wrigley mansion, now "Tournament House" and headquarters of the Pasadena Rose Tournament Association, for a guided tour (391 S. Orange Grove Boulevard, Pasadena; 818/449-4100). In the Spring, take time for a stroll through the rose gardens.

47. Study Pasadena architecture on a tour of the Gamble House designed by the Greene brothers (4 Westmorland Place, parallel to the 300 block of N. Orange Grove; 818/793-3334); "La Miniatura" by Frank Lloyd Wright (645 Prospect Crescent); the Grace Nicholson home, now the Pacific Asia Museum (46 N. Los Robles; 818/449-2742); the restored "La Casita" (177 S. Arroyo Boulevard) and Rose Bowl by Myron Hunt; and the Art Center College of Design (1700 Lida Street in the Linda Vista area west of the Rose Bowl) by Craig Elwood. Following lunch at the Caltech Athenaeum on Hill Street (818/793-6146), designed by Gordon Kaufman, the Pasadena Historical Society could be invited to present a slide show on early Pasadena (818/577-1660).

48. Take the Pasadena Heritage tour of 38 historic bungalow courts, or any of their other tours; self-guided tour brochures are available (80 W. Dayton Street; 818/793-0617).

Arrange for lunch at the *Beaux-Arts* Feynes Mansion, 470 W. Walnut at Orange Grove (Pasadena Historical Society: 818/577-1660). Invite a speaker from the Society, or from the Pasadena Urban Conservation Office, Pasadena City Hall, 100 N. Garfield, Pasadena, CA 91101.

49. Find history in the foothills, including Upton Sinclair's home at 464 N. Myrtle, and the 1886 George Anderson house at 215 E. Lime (Monrovia Historical Society:

818/358-3129). Other sites include the Aztec Hotel at 311 W. Foothill near Magnolia, and "The Oaks" at 250 N. Primrose. Contact the Monrovia Old House Preservation Committee (702 E. Foothill Boulevard, Monrovia, CA 91016) for tours and tour brochures on the historic homes in the area.

50. In Sierra Madre see the world's largest wisteria, and view the 1887 Pinney house at 225 Lime Street, the 1870s Richardson house at 167 E. Mira Monte and the 1880s Lizzie's Trail Inn next door, at the foot of the Mt. Wilson Trail. The Sierra Madre Historical Society (P.O. Box 202, Sierra Madre, CA 91024) has a brochure on the community's historic buildings.

Proceed to the Duarte Historical Museum, a ten-room house exhibiting local memorabilia (located in Encanto Park, 377 Encanto Parkway, Duarte; 818/357-9419).

51. Visit the Scripps Home built at the turn of the century, now a retirement home, at 2212 N. El Molino, Altadena (818/798-0934). Drive by Chateau Bradbury, designed by Robert Farquhar and built by developer Lewis L. Bradbury for his daughter, on California Street in Monrovia. Proceed to Slauson Park in Azusa, built in just one day (320 N. Orange Place), and visit the Lindley Scott home (720 E. Foothill Boulevard) and the impressive Slauson home, now Manressa Retreat House (18337 E. Foothill; 818/969-1848).

Lunch in Glendora at the Continental Restaurant, built around the 1880s Shank Home, 316 W. Alosta. Stop at Memlin House, presently the state headquarters for the Daughters of the American Revolution (201 W. Bennet; 818/963-1776, 335-5407). Conclude with a visit to the Glendora Historical Museum, housed in the old fire station building at 314 N. Glendora Avenue (Glendora Historical Society: 818/335-4071).

52. As guests of the Arroyo Seco Ranger District (818/792-1151), take a daylong outing to Sturtevant Camp, first established in 1893 by Sierra Madre resident Wilbur Sturtevant. Along the way view the 50-foot Sturtevant Falls located 1-1/2 miles by trail from the Chantry Flats parking lot. Request a talk by a U.S. Forest Ranger describing the history of local mountaineering and health resorts in Santa Anita Canyon at the turn of the century (818/574-5272; 818/358-9162).

53. Using a road atlas as a guide, tour a portion of historic Route 66, used by immigrants to California during the Depression Era and Dust Bowl days. Follow Foothill Boulevard to Monrovia, the county's fourth-oldest city; note the unusual Aztec Hotel, built in 1926 at the intersection of Foothill and Magnolia. Foothill Boulevard ends at Mountain Avenue; go south on Mountain, then east on Huntington through Duarte; Huntington will become Foothill again as you pass through the outskirts of Irwindale. Continue along Foothill through Azusa and Glendora, where Foothill jogs south again; take Amelia Avenue to Alosta/Foothill and continue east through San Dimas to La Verne. Follow on through a portion of Pomona to Claremont, home of the Claremont Colleges, where you might visit Rancho Santa Ana Botanic Gardens. On the southwest corner at intersection with Indian Hill, note the building of native rock, once a garage and service station; there are many old houses using native boulders in these foothill communities.

As you proceed along Foothill beyond Claremont, you leave Los Angeles County and enter San Bernardino County. Continue on Foothill to Euclid in Upland, where the grassy median strip was used for the annual All States Picnics. At the intersection, representing the crossing of four overland routes, the Daughters of the American Revolution have installed a statue, "Madonna of the Trail," dedicated to pioneer mothers. Next comes Rancho Cucamonga, where you may wish to pause for a meal at the Sycamore Inn, 8318 Foothill Boulevard (714/982-1104); once a Butterfield Stage stop, it was built in 1848. Continue through Fontana and Rialto, where you will note the old Virginia Dare Winery building on the north side of the highway. Don't miss the famous Wigwam Motel 2728 at W. Foothill in Rialto.

From San Bernardino, Route 66 follows the Cajon Pass through the San Bernardino Mountains to Victorville and Barstow, then follows the National Trails Highway to Needles, last city on the California side of the Colorado River border with Arizona.

E. San Gabriel Valley & East:

The arrival of the emigrants in El Monte gave the first decided impulse to agriculture in this county, encouraged business in the city of Los Angeles, and ever since has aided it materially. This great farming tract lies along the San Gabriel River, twelve miles east of the city. The soil in general does not need irrigation.

Col. J.J. Warner, Judge Benjamin Hayes and Dr. J.P. Widney, *An Historical Sketch of Los Angeles County, California* (1876).

54. Relive the days of the ranchos with a brief visit to the Meredith Adobe, the restored W.R. Rowland Ranch foreman's house, constructed of adobe and redwood (in Lemon Creek Park, 130 Avenida Alipaz, Walnut).

Proceed to the *Italianate* Victorian (1875) Louis Phillips Mansion, 2640 Pomona Boulevard (714/622-2043). View the historic Barbara Greenwood Kindergarten on the adjacent property, at McKinley & Hacienda, and visit the old Spadra Cemetery next to 2882 Pomona Boulevard. Follow with a tour of restored Casa Primera, headquarters of the Historical Society of Pomona Valley (714/629-7511). Following a self-guided tour of the Adobe de Palomares, enjoy box lunches under the grape arbor (491 E. Arrow Highway; 714/620-2300).

Proceed to the annual celebration of Rancho Days held each May at Casa de Rancho Cucamonga (714/989-1858).

55. Visit the John A. Rowland Home (interior presently closed for earthquake repair) and tour the adjoining Rowland-Dibble Museum. John Rowland's granddaughter, Lillian Dibble, converted a water tank to house a museum devoted to pioneer life (16021 E. Gale Avenue, City of Industry; La Puente Valley Historical Society: 818/336-2382). Pay a visit to the museum of the Chino Historical Society, 5493 B Street (P.O. Box 972, Chino, CA 91708; 714/629-2301). Proceed to the Yorba-Slaughter Adobe, 17127 Pomona-Rincon Road, Chino (714/597-2611). The two-acre complex includes a winery and ranch building containing hundreds of period items.

56. Tour the San Bernardino County Museum at 2024 Orange Tree Lane (714/792-1334), and lunch at the adjacent Edwards Mansion, 2064 Orange Tree Lane, Redlands (714/793-2031). Take the Alabama Street offramp north from the I-10 freeway, west of downtown Redlands. Proceed to the Casa de Rancho Cucamonga/Rains Home, a southern mansion built in 1858 (8810 Hemlock Street, Rancho Cucamonga; 714/989-4970).

57. Explore San Gabriel Valley history with a visit to the Alhambra Historical Society Museum, 1550 W. Alhambra Road (818/300-8845). Visit Dinsmoor Heritage House (9632 Steele Street, Rosemead, CA 91770-1505) and the Richardson Farmhouse, a frequent movie location site, on Mission Drive in Rosemead.

Plan box lunches to be enjoyed at the Log Cabin, 3535 Santa Anita Avenue, El Monte (818/580-2200). Or stop at In-and-Out Burgers, the first drive-through fast food restaurant in Southern California (13502 E. Virginia Avenue, Baldwin Park).

Visit the Covina Valley Historical Society Museum in the old jail at 125 E. College in Covina, and proceed to the Society's Heritage House at 300 N. Valencia Street, where tours are available (818/332-1429).

58. Take a walking tour sponsored by Claremont Heritage (714/621-0848), with visits to the Santa Fe Railroad Station, the Francis Bacon Library and the Kenneth G. Fiske Museum of Musical Instruments, 450 College Way (by appointment only: 714/621-8307).

Visit the Padua Hills Theatre (owned by Pomona College: 714/621-8000). Stop at the Webb School to visit the Raymond M. Alf Museum and the stunning mission-style chapel set upon the crest of the hill (1175 Base Line Road, Claremont, CA 91711; 714/624-2798).

F. Westside:

> *As I sat there on that ancient bench, . . . I surrendered to the illusion. The sky was blue. A slow wind came up from the bay, moving through the surrounding screen of eucalyptus, sycamore and cypress. The bronze youth dozing in the pool was a slave; he would soon be awakened by his master's whistle. It was a nice day in Herculaneum, summer of '74.*

Jack Smith, "The Getty Museum and the Assyrian Rubber Factory," *Jack Smith's L.A.* (1980).

59. Take a tour of L.A. County's Virginia Robinson Gardens, three blocks north of Sunset Boulevard on Elden Way in Bel Air (310/446-8251), followed by a tour of Greystone Park's 18-1/2 acres of formal gardens located at 501 Doheny Road & Loma Vista Drive in Beverly Hills. Stop at the historic Beverly Hills Hotel on Sunset at Benedict Canyon Drive for a coffee break.

60. Visit the historic Centinela Adobe, 7634 Midfield Avenue, Westchester, and tour the home built by Jose Ygnacio Machado in 1833-34. The complex also includes the original Centinela-Inglewood Land Company office building of the booming 1880s, now a museum, and the History Research Center which contains the reassembled library from "Centinela," the residence of Inglewood city founder Daniel Freeman, several display cases of changing exhibits, an extensive photographic collection and a huge closet of vintage clothing (Historical Society of Centinela Valley: 310/649-6272).

61. Visit Will Rogers State Historic Park, 14253 Sunset Boulevard (310/454-8212). Take a walking tour (Neighborhood Place Project, 8571-1/4 Rugby Drive, West Hollywood, CA 90069; 310/657-3733) of nearby Uplifters Ranch, laid out in 1914, in the dense groves of the nation's first experimental forestry station. Note particularly the three log cabins at 36, 37 and 38 Haldeman Road, which were obtained from the set of the silent film, *The Courtship of Miles Standish.* Consult Gebhard & Winter, *Architecture in Los Angeles: A Compleat Guide,* p. 45.

62. Examine three architectural innovations: visit the Mutual Housing Association, Henly Avenue at Rochedale Way, planned by Contini, Jones, *et al.* Proceed to the Strathmore Apts. at 11005 West Strathmore, Westwood where Neutra gave a *Modern* interpretation to the bungalow court, and also visit the Kelton, Elkay and Landfair apartments as well as Lautner's Sheets Apts. Proceed to Pacific Palisades and the Case Study House Project, including the Eames House & Studio at 203 Chautauqua Boulevard and others at 199 and 205. Consult Gebhard & Winter, *Architecture in Los Angeles: A Compleat Guide*, pp. 116-133.

63. Explore UCLA's many resources with a campus tour. Guided tours begin from the Visitors Center, #1417 Uberroth Building, 10945 Le Conte Avenue, (310/206-8147). Shuttle service is available. Take time to explore the Fowler Museum of Natural History (310/206-1459).

Notes

G. Port & Beach Cities:

. . . There stands Los Angeles, which dug a harbor by its bootstraps and filled it with world commerce. More than water was needed to do that.

Saturday Evening Post Editorial, April 1, 1939.

64. Tour the *Queen Mary* at Pier J in Long Beach (310/435-3511), and invite a speaker from the Steamship Historical Society (351 S. Fuller Avenue #8-J, Los Angeles, CA 90036) or from the Historical Society of Long Beach (P.O. Box 1869, Long Beach, CA 90801-1869; 310/435-7511). Also visit Howard Hughes' giant airplane, the "Spruce Goose" (310/435-3511).

In the afternoon, take a Long Beach Harbor cruise (310/514-3838).

65. In San Pedro visit the Cabrillo Marine Museum (3720 Stephen White Drive; 310/831-3207). Also tour the Los Angeles Maritime Museum, housed in the old San Pedro Ferry Building at the foot of 6th Street, Berth 84 (310/546-7618). The *S.S. Lane Victory*, a World War II Victory ship built in San Pedro, may be visited at Berth 53. Tour the Muller House museum at 1542 S. Beacon Street (San Pedro Bay Historical Society; 310/548-3208), and the historic Point Fermin Lighthouse, a unique 19th-century structure (Point Fermin Park, Gaffey Street and Paseo del Mar; 310/548-7756). Mary Smith was the first lighthouse keeper here in 1874.

An interesting side excursion could be made to the Palos Verdes Peninsula to visit what remains of the Radio Ranch, located at the corner of Highridge and Armaga Springs Roads. A museum is planned on the site to commemorate the half-century the area served as an international short wave and amateur radio station.

Round out the day with a sunset cruise (one of several possibilities is Spirit Adventures: 310/831-1075).

66. Visit the Redondo Beach Historical Museum (320 Knob Hill; 310/372-1171) as guests of that Historical Society. Proceed to the renovated Firehouse Museum (2103 Havemeyer Street) with its remarkable collection of antique fire engines and equipment. Tour the historic district -- the 300 block of N. Gertruda, the 400 block of Emerald, and the 400-800 blocks of El Redondo still accented with the original gas lamps.

In Manhattan Beach visit the original beach cottage in Pollywog Park (Manhattan Beach Boulevard at Redondo Avenue) and the old pier currently undergoing restoration (end of Manhattan Beach Boulevard).

67. As guests of the Venice Historical Society (P.O. Box 2012, Venice, CA 90294) and the Venice Canals Homeowners Association (310/832-5516) visit the remaining canals originally created by Abbot Kinney early in this century. The visit should include stops at Bungalow Island with its remaining ten bungalows dating from 1925, and at The Arches, 1516 Pacific, one of the first (1905) arched buildings constructed by Kinney.

68. Sail the *Catalina Express* to Catalina Island (Catalina Terminal, Box 1391, San Pedro, CA 90733; 310/519-1212). Visit the Catalina Island Museum, downstairs in the Casino Building (Catalina Island Museum Society, P.O. Box 366, Avalon, Catalina Island, CA 90704-0366; 310/510-2414). Take a guided tour of the historic Casino. Tour the Wrigley Memorial & Botanical Garden at the head of Avalon Canyon (310/510-2288). Visit the Hopi-style pueblo built in 1926 as a private home for author Zane Grey, and now a hotel (199 Chimes Tower Road; 310/510-0966, 510-0966). Arrange a tour of the museum in 1890 Holly Hill House, a private residence located on a hill above Avalon Bay (consult Catalina Island Museum Society, above). Also visit Mt. Ida, William Wrigley Jr.'s classic 1921 summer home, now a bed & breakfast inn (310/510-2030).

22

H. Whittier & South:

The city bakes in an amber coastal plain, shut off from the world by a horseshoe of mountains to the north, east, and south, and by an ocean to the westward. The city is . . . Los Angeles, U.S.A., amid its litter of tributary towns.

Paul Hollister, "Walt Disney," *The Atlantic Monthly*, December 1940.

69. Visit the impressive three-story Whittier Historical Museum (6755 Newlin Street, Whittier; 310/945-3871) and the Joshua Baily House Museum and Park (13421 E. Camilla Street; 310/696-9048). Nearby is the Los Angeles County Sheriffs Museum, 11515 S. Colima Road at Telegraph Boulevard (310/946-7081).

70. Spend the day in Norwalk at the six-acre Paddison Farm, with its 1878 Victorian house and ranch complex; arrange to picnic on the grounds (11951 Imperial Highway; 310/864-1407). Visit the Johnson-Hargitt House Museum, 12436 Mapledale Street, and the Gilbert Sproul Museum, 12237 Sproul Street, both in Norwalk (310/864-9663).

71. Take a guided tour of six-acre Heritage Park, Norwalk Boulevard & Telegraph Road in Santa Fe Springs (310/946-6476), to see a 4000-square-foot Victorian carriage-barn/museum, formal gardens, a tank house, an aviary and a conservatory, as well as two archaeological excavation sites. Picnic tables are available on the park grounds.
Visit the Marie Rankin Clark Estate designed by Irving Gill, off Pioneer Boulevard south of Telegraph Road (310/863-4896, 863-4898), and the Hathaway Ranch Museum, 11901 E. Florence Avenue (310/944-6563)

72. Tour the Woodworth Home Museum, home of the Bell Gardens Historical Society, 6821 Fosterbridge Boulevard, Bell Gardens.
Take a walking tour of historic Gallatin, today's Downey, including Gallatin School, the Neighbors home and the elegant 1910 Rives home at 3rd and Paramount. A

brochure is available from the Downey Historical Society outlining the self-guided tour (Downey History Center, 12540 Rives Avenue; 310/862-2777). Picnic on park grounds, or have lunch at the oldest existing, original MacDonald's (1953), 10207 Lakewood Boulevard.

Visit the Carpenter's House museum, 10500 E. Flora Vista, Bellflower (310/867-2212).

Notes

Orange County

Within the next few years the horticultural industry of Orange County will assume proportions that will astonish even the most sanguine. Already the keynote has been sounded, the "horny-handed sons of toil" have awakened from their slumber and with thoughts of coming wealth, with all its luxuries and pleasures, are working as they never worked before. Acres upon acres of the county's favorite soil are being planted to trees of every description and an air of prosperity is pervading homes of our honest and faithful husbandmen.

Santa Ana Board of Trade, 1891.

73. A visit to Anaheim could include a stop at the Peralta Adobe built by Ramon Peralta in 1871 (SW corner Fairmont and Santa Ana Canyon Road). Visit the 1857-58 Mother Colony House, the small redwood *Greek Revival* residence of George Hansen, who supervised the development of the Los Angeles Vineyard Company; in 1929 it became the county's first historical museum (414 N. West Street; 714/774-3840). Tour Red Cross House, an excellent example of Victorian *Queen Ann* elegance (418 N. West Street: 714/778-4526).

Lunch at the White House Restaurant in the historic Truxaw-Gervais House (887 S. Anaheim Boulevard; 714/630-2812). In the afternoon, visit the Anaheim Museum in the old Carnegie Library (241 S. Anaheim Boulevard; 714/778-3301). If time allows, visit the historic Anaheim Cemetery at 1400 E. Sycamore Street (714/535-4928).

74. In Santa Ana, visit the 1889 Howe-Waffle House & Medical Museum, the two-story *Queen Anne* style home of Dr. Willella Waffle (120 Civic Center Drive West; 714/543-3086, 549-2857). A brief walk leads to the impressively restored Old Orange County Courthouse Museum, built of Arizona red sandstone (211 W. Santa Ana Boulevard; 714/834-5536). Proceed to the Charles W. Bowers Memorial Museum (2002 N. Main Street; 714/972-1900), which houses a wealth of historical material in *Spanish Colonial* buildings. The Discovery Museum of Orange County is a hands-on history museum which helps visitors experience life at the turn of the century; it is located in the restored home of Hiram Clay Kellogg (3101 W. Harvard Street; 714/540-0404).

75. An Orange County museum tour could begin with Red Car Heritage Square, where Pacific Electric Car #1734, serves as headquarters of the Seal Beach Historical & Cultural Society and a museum of early Orange County history (707 Electric Avenue at Main Street, "Old Town" Seal Beach; 310/596-2579). Visit the International Museum of Graphic Communication, which highlights significant stages in the development of printing (8469 Kass Drive, Buena Park; 714/523-2070). Also visit the Westminster Museum, which documents the efforts of Rev. Lemuel Weber to establish the community as a temperance settlement in 1870 (14102 Hoover Street, Westminster; 714/891-1126).

Continue to the Costa Mesa Historical Society Museum, which traces the history of the community originally known as "Harper," as well as the story of the Santa Ana Army Air Base (corner of Anaheim Avenue and Plumer Street: 714/631-5918). In nearby Estancia Park stands the restored three-room Diego Sepulveda Adobe, built in the early 1800s (1900 Adams Avenue, Costa Mesa; 714/631-5918).

76. Visit the Irvine Historical Museum, which highlights the importance of both cattle and lima beans in the region's development (5 San Joaquin at Sandburg Way, behind the golf course parking lot). Join the Irvine Historical Society for a three-hour bus tour of the Irvine Ranch and Old Town Irvine, including the La Quinta Hotel, built around the original bean silos (Society & Museum: 714/786-4112).

The trip could include a stop at Newland House, a thirteen-room *Queen Ann* Victorian (19820 Beach Boulevard at Adams Avenue, Huntington Beach; 714/962-5777).

77. Take a southern tour of California Victorians including the 1870 Gilbert Sproul Museum in Norwalk (310/864-9663), the 1880s Bacon cabin and the Whitaker-Jaunes home in Buena Park (Buena Park Historical Society: 714/521-9900).

Visit the Talbert Real Estate Office and a Japanese Bath House and Tank House at 17641 Los Alamos, Fountain Valley (Fountain Valley Historical Society, P.O. Box 8592, Fountain Valley, CA 92708). The Tustin Area Mu seum, 395 El Camino Real in Tustin, is maintained by the Tustin Area Historical Society (P.O. Box 185, Tustin, CA 92683; 714/891-1126).

78. Celebrate the place of citrus in Orange County's development with a visit to the Santiago Orange Growers Association Packing House, one of the few still operating in the county (350 N. Cypress Street, Orange). Also visit the Ainsworth Historical House, restored to reflect the style of the early 1900s (414 E. Chapman Avenue, Orange; 714/532-0380). Nearby is the Plaza Historic District, with over fifty buildings of architectural interest (intersection of Chapman Avenue and Glassell Street). Lunch at Watson's Drug Store, established in 1899 and still a popular lunch spot (116 E. Chapman Avenue). A self-guided walking tour brochure of the City of Orange is available from the Orange Chamber of Commerce, 80 Plaza Square (714/538-3581).

On return to Los Angeles County visit Bradford House, 136 W. Palm Circle in Placentia, built by early citrus promoter Albert S. Bradford (Placentia Founders Society: 714/993-2470). If time permits, visit Heritage Park, 12174 Euclid Street in Garden Grove, a ten-acre site which includes the authentically furnished Stanley House, a windmill and tank house, and a replica of Garden Grove's first fire station (Garden Grove Historical Society: 714/530-8871).

79. Tour the authentically-furnished Heritage House (Clark House, an 1894 *Eastlake*-style Victorian) and Arboretum on the campus of CSU Fullerton, Yorba Linda Boulevard and Associated Road. Proceed to the Key Ranch, the Victorian home of citrus pioneer George Key, where citrus trees, memorabilia and a remarkable collection of farm equipment document the history of citriculture in Orange County (625 W. Bastanchury Road, Placentia: 714/528-4260).

Lunch at Bessie Wall's, 1074 N. Tustin Avenue, Anaheim (714/630-2812). Proceed to the nine-acre Richard Nixon Library and Birthplace complex, 18001 Yorba Linda Boulevard (714/993-3393). Also make a stop at the first school house in Yorba Linda at 4866 Olinda Street.

80. Take a five-block walking tour of historic Fullerton (714/992-6882). Visit the Fullerton Museum at

301 N. Pomona Avenue; originally funded by the WPA, it served as the city's library for 30 years before becoming a museum in 1941 (714/738-6545). Also visit the Amerige Brothers Real Estate Office Museum at 340 W. Commonwealth Avenue.

Lunch in a restored 1918 *Mission Revival* Pacific Electric depot at 128 E. Commonwealth Avenue. Or stop at the restaurant in the 1923 *Mission Revival* Union Pacific Depot at 110 E. Santa Fe, next to the 1930 *Spanish Colonial* Santa Fe Depot which today serves as Fullerton's Amtrak station.

81. Plan a trip to Heritage Hill Historic Park, near Forest Lake Drive and Serrano Road in El Toro and tour its four restored structures: the 1863 Serrano Adobe, the 1891 St. George's Episcopal Mission, the 1890 El Toro Grammar School and the 1908 Bennet Ranch House. Ask for a docent demonstration of the imaginative schoolhouse program offered to touring 4th grade students (714/855-2028).

82. Visit that incredible antique shop, Libros y Artes, in San Juan Capistrano. Tour Mission San Juan Capistrano (714/493-1424), where the 1797-1806 stone church is in ruins but the 1778 Serra Chapel has been lovingly restored. Follow with a visit to the imposing St. John's Church, a larger-scale replica of the original mission church and bell tower, decorated by art historian Norman Neuerburg. Tour the Harrison House/Parra Adobe on Ortega Highway and the restored Montanez Adobe (Cultural Arts & Heritage Commission: 714/493-1171). Join a guided historical walking tour (San Juan Capistrano Historical Society: 714/493-8444).

San Bernardino & Riverside Counties

Redlands, San Bernardino County, shares honors with Riverside, Riverside County, as premier city of the citrus belt. Founded in March 1887 on the sloping hillside that formed the southern edge of the San Bernardino Valley, eighty miles inland from the sea. Redlands had become by the early 1900s a city of distinctive public buildings in Mission revival or Romanesque . . . and gracious bungalows on broad streets shaded by pepper and palm, possessed on its western edge of a view across the orange-grove-carpeted San Bernardino Valley and to the east, the snow-capped peaks of the Sierra Madre, dominated by hoary Mount San Bernardino.

Kevin Starr, *Inventing the Dream: California Through the Progressive Era* (1985).

83. Visit the favorite getaways of 1920s Hollywood with stops at W.K. Kellogg's mansion and Arabian horse ranch on the campus of Cal Poly Pomona at 3801 W. Temple (714/869-3378), and Pomona's Fox Theatre at 114 W. 3rd Street (714/622-8778), where previews were shown. Then visit Riverside's famed Mission Inn as guests of the Mission Inn Restoration Foundation (714/781-8241).

Return via Norco, with a stop at Lake Norconia and an arranged lunch stop at the Naval Weapons Station dining room, the former ballroom of Rex Clark's lakeside Norconia Resort Casino of the 1920s. The property is now divided into a State rehabilitation center for narcotics users, and the Corona Annex of the Naval Weapons Center (Department of the Navy, NWAC, Corona, CA 91720-5000; 714/736-5000).

84. Tour the four-story California Museum of Photography located in downtown Riverside along the Main Street Pedestrian Mall, 3824 Main Street (714/787-4787). The 800-square-foot exhibition traces the history of photography; lectures and films are presented in the auditorium. Allow time for a visit to the Jensen-Alvarado Ranch Historic Park, site of the oldest house in Riverside, at 4350 Riverside Drive (714/787-2551).

In nearby Redlands visit the *Mission Revival* Holt House, 405 W. Olive; the elaborate Morey House, 140 Terracina; and Kimberly Crest, 1325 Prospect Drive (714/792-2111), California mansion of the Kimberly-Clark paper goods magnate. Also tour the *Asistencia Mision de San Gabriel*, where there are two museums within the whitewashed structure built in 1830 (26930 Barton Road; 714/793-5402).

Brochures, listing additional historic buildings in Riverside and giving locations of some of the many Victorian homes for which Redlands is noted, are listed under Self Guided Tours in Appendix A.

85. History in the mountains: visit the Big Bear Historical Museum (P.O. Box 513, Big Bear City, CA 92314; 714/585-8100). Or join Friends of Big Bear Valley Preserve in a two-day spring trek which begins at Horse House, at the north end of Baldwin Lake, and includes the historic gold mining areas of Holcomb Valley (P.O. Box 1418, Sugarloaf, CA 92386; 818/357-3542).

86. In Palm Springs, visit Village Green Heritage Center at South Palm Canyon Drive at Tahquitz-McCallum Way (619/327-2156), which includes the Cornelia White House, Ruddy's General Store Museum and the McCallum Adobe featuring changing photo exhibits presented by the Palm Springs Historical Society (P.O. Box 1498, Palm Springs, CA 92262). The Desert Museum houses art collections and natural history exhibits. Visit four-acre Moorton Botanical Garden, with its amazing collection of 2,000 varieties of desert plants from many parts of the world.

87. View the spring appleblossoms or gather autumn apples in the twelve orchards in Oak Glen (Yucaipa Valley Chamber of Commerce, P.O. Box 35, Yucaipa, CA 92399; 714/790-1841). The 1927 Oak Glen School House has been restored to its original state, and is now a museum of historical memorabilia. Lunch at any of the several restaurants on Oak Glen Road -- most offer fresh-baked apple pie for dessert.

Visit the 1842 Diego Sepulveda House Museum/Yucaipa Adobe at 32183 Kentucky Street in Yucaipa (714/795-3485) and the Mousley Museum of Natural History, purported to house the largest collection of seashells in the United States (35350 Panorama Drive, Yucaipa; 714/797-1511). Tour the Edward Dean Museum of Decorative Arts at 9401 Oak Glen Road, Cherry Valley (714/845-2626).

88. Visit the Coachella Valley Museum & Cultural Center in Indio, housed in the 1926 home of Harry "Doc" Smiley, a Valley pioneer medical practitioner. Exhibits include antique agricultural equipment, Native American artifacts and other historical items including an archive of memoirs and county records. Note the "submarine" -- a model of a one-room dwelling used by railroad workers, designed to shield them from the desert sun. There are three gardens associated with the museum: a rose garden, a desert garden and an authentic Japanese garden (82-616 Miles Avenue at Deglet Noor, Indio; 619/342-6651).

You may wish to schedule your Indio visit to coincide with the National Date Festival in February. This county fair with an Arabian Nights theme includes local produce exhibits, notably Coachella grapefruit and other citrus, and many varieties of dates (619/342-8247).

Notes

San Diego & Imperial Counties

Within the grove was a variety of shrubs and odoriferous plants, as the Rosemary, the Sage, Roses of Castile, and above all a quantity of wild grapevines, which at the time were in blossom. The country was of joyous appearance, and the lands contiguous to the river appeared of excellent friableness, and capable of producing every species of fruits.

From Miguel Costanso, *Narrative of the Portola Expedition.*

89. Travel south to San Pasqual Battlefield State Historic Park (619/238-3380, 489-0076) on Highway 78 east of the San Diego Wild Animal Park. An April tour could include the annual rodeo at Woodside, twenty miles northeast of San Diego on Hwy. 8.

The return trip might include a stop at the Antique Convertible Car Museum (Deer Park: Vintage Cars & Wines) with more than fifty cars from the early 1900s through the 1950s, located at 29013 Champagne Boulevard, Escondido. The Lawrence Welk Museum of the entertainer's memorabilia can be reached from the same freeway exit (8860 Lawrence Welk Drive (619/749-3448). Time permitting, visit one or more of Temecula's wineries, such as Callaway at 32720 Rancho California Road (714/676-4001) or Mount Palomar at 33820 Rancho California Road (714/676-5047).

90. Have a north San Diego County adventure, stopping first at Lake Elsinor off I-15. Proceed south to Julian and the 100-year-old Julian Hotel at 2032 Main Street (619/765-0201), the Pioneer Museum at 2811 Washington Street, and the Eagle and High Peak Gold Mines (619/765-0036) and Miner's Camp (619/765-1020). Julian has a Wildflower Show every spring, and a fall celebration of the apple harvest (Julian Chamber of Commerce: 619/765-1857).

Proceed north to Mission San Antonio de Pala (north of SR 76 on Pala Mission Road; 619/742-3317) and the 12,000-acre Pala Indian Reservation and Cupa Cultural Center; an annual Corpus Christi fiesta is held in early June. Return by way of Fallbrook, lunching at La Caseta on N. Vine Street (619/728-9737). Following lunch, browse through the antique shops along the main street.

91. Take a trip to the threshing bee and antique engine show in the spring or fall at the Southwestern Antique Gas & Steam Engine Museum (619/941-1791, 310/834-6007), 2040 N. Santa Fe Drive, in Rancho Guajome Regional Park. Also in the 45-acre Park is a partially restored hacienda, chapel and cemetery (2210 N. Santa Fe Drive, Vista; 619/565-3600).

Include a visit to Escondido's Grape Day Park with its Heritage Walk, a group of early buildings restored to serve as a museum complex (on Broadway, between Washington Avenue and Valley Parkway; 619/743-8207).

92. Attend the mid-July fiesta at Mission San Luis Rey de Francia, located four miles east of Oceanside on SR 76 (619/757-3651).

93. Travel along the coast to north San Diego County stopping at the restored 1887 Magee House once owned by Florence Magee, an early member of this settlement of German and Bohemian families (258 Beech Avenue, Carlsbad; 619/434-2855). Visit the Self-Realization Fellowship Garden (215 K Street, Encinitas; 619/753-1811), and Quail Botanical Gardens on Quail Gardens Drive, Encinitas (619/436-3036).

Lunch in Rancho Santa Fe at The Inn (Linea del Cielo at Paseo Delicias; 619/756-1131). The Country Friends Shop -- don't miss the Annex -- has many fine antiques (6030 El Tordo; 619/756-1192).

94. In San Diego take a self-guided walking tour of Golden Hill-Sherman Heights, or of the Gas Lamp District (tour brochures from San Diego Historical Society, P.O. Box 81825, San Diego, CA 92138; 619/297-3258). Visit the 1904-06 George Marston House at 3525 7th Street (619/298-3142), and note neighboring houses at 3526 7th (1906) and 3575 7th (1909), also by Irving Gill. Tour the immense 1887 *Queen Anne* mansion, Villa Montezuma/Jesse Sheppard House (1925 K Street 619/239-2211), and the William Heath Davis House (619/233-5227). Lunch at the restored Horton Hotel.

Stop in Coronado at the Glorietta Bay Inn built in 1908 by John D. Spreckels (619/435-3101), and take a self-guided tour of the 1888 Hotel Del Coronado (1500 Orange Avenue, Coronado, CA 92118; 619/522-8011); then drive through the picturesque beach community. Dine at the Chart House (1701 Strand Way in Coronado; 619/435-0155), an 1887 *Eastlake* Victorian boat-house with a view of Glorietta Bay. For further information contact: Coronado Visitor Information, P.O. Box 181173, Coronado, CA 92118-1173; 1-800/622-8300.

95. Visit the Cabrillo National Monument on Catalina Boulevard at the end of Point Loma (619/293-5450) to witness the reenactment of the 1542 landing of Juan Rodriguez Cabrillo, part of San Diego's annual Cabrillo festival held in late September (619/557-5040). While there, stop at the visitors' center and museum located in the nearby Old Point Loma Lighthouse which was in operation from 1855 to 1891.

96. Tour the San Diego Railroad Museum at Campo in eastern San Diego County. Take a scenic 15-mile train ride, examine more than 50 pieces of rail equipment, and visit the 103-year old Campo Stone Store, headquarters of the Mountain Empire Historical Society (P.O. Box 394, Campo, CA 92006; 619/697-7762, 478-9937).

Visit the San Diego Model Railroad Museum, which contains four scale-model layouts depicting the geography and historical development of southern California railroading (Casa de Balboa building, Balboa Park, San Diego; 619/696-0199). Note the Botanical Building across the street, a reassembled Santa Fe Railroad station.

97. Tour the Junipero Serra Museum on the hill at 2727 Presidio Drive (619/297-3258), and take a walking tour of San Diego Old Town State Historic Park; a daily guided tour and brochures for a self-guided tour are available from the Visitor Center (619/237-6770). The Park includes the Plaza, the 1824-1830 Alvarado House, the 1860s Black Hawk Smithy & Stable, the 1860s Johnson House, 1827 La Casa de Estudillo, the 1865 Mason Street School, the 1853 two-story adobe Robinson-Rose House, the San Diego Union Museum, and the Seeley Stables housing a collection of horse-drawn vehicles. Visit the 1856-57 *Greek Revival* Whaley House (restored 1956), considered to be to be the first two-story brick home in southern California (2482 San Diego Avenue; 619/298-2482) and the Wells

Fargo History Museum, a recreated express office of the 1850s.

98. On the San Diego waterfront, visit the Maritime Museum at 1306 N. Harbor Drive (619/234-9153), consisting of three historic vessels: the 1863 tall ship *Star of India*, the 1898 ferry *Berkeley* and the 1904 steam yacht *Medea*. Lunch on a lavish seafood buffet at Anthony's Harborside, 1355 Harbor Drive overlooking the harbor (619/232-6358).

Tour Mission Basilica San Diego de Alcala, 10818 San Diego Mission Road on the north side of Mission Valley (619/281-8449). The first of Alta California's missions, it was founded July 16, 1769 and relocated to its present site in 1774.

99. Visit the Imperial Valley Pioneers Museum on the Imperial County Fairgrounds (204 E. 2nd Street off Imperial Avenue, Imperial; 619/355-1222). Learn the story of the pioneering farmers, ranchers and dairymen who settled the valley, and see the fine collection of their agricultural implements. Exhibits include a number of early carts and buggies, and displays on the development of the Valley's irrigation. Contact the Imperial Valley Historical Society, Box 224, Imperial, CA 92251. The California Mid-Winter Fair is held on the Fairgrounds in February (619/355-1181).

Imperial Valley's agriculture has given rise to a series of special celebrations where farmers proudly display their produce, both "in the raw" and used in an imaginative array of original recipes. There are associated activities ranging from parades and beauty contests to carnivals and even a tractor pull. Holtville's Carrot Festival is in January (619/356-2923), Niland's Tomato Festival follows in February (619/348-0546), and El Centro proudly hosts the Imperial Sweet Onion Festival in May (619/353-1900).

100. The Desert Cavalcade in Calexico each March celebrates the arrival of de Anza in the Imperial Valley: grand parade, food booths and *folklorico* dancing to traditional Mexican music (619/357-1166). Prepare for your visit with a presentation on de Anza.

Santa Barbara County

Because the California coast veered sharply in an east-west direction below Point Conception . . . Santa Barbara faced south, not west, and was thus protected by mountains from the wind and fogs of the coast. Uniquely situated, Santa Barbara possessed a steadily sunny micro-climate perfect for recovering invalids. Santa Barbara was also blessed with a number of mineral springs in the city itself, in nearby Montecito and near the Arroyo Burro on former Mission property. By the late 1870s bottled Veronica Water from the Arroyo Burro springs, known for its gently laxative effects . . . was bringing the reputation of Santa Barbara as a health resort to the apothecary shops of the nation.

Kevin Starr, *Material Dreams: Southern California Through the 1920s* (1990).

101. In Santa Barbara take the 14-block "Red Tile Walking Tour" (maps at Visitor Center, 1 Santa Barbara Street; 805/965-3021). Note the Carrillo Adobe, where Rafaela Ortega, descendant of the first Presidio *comandante*, lived in 1826. Include antique shopping in the old houses on Brinkerhoff Avenue between Cota and Haley Streets. Stop for high tea at the Four Seasons Biltmore, 1260 Channel Drive (805/969-2261) and dinner at the Plow and Angel located in a stone-built 19th-century citrus packing plant at the San Ysidro Ranch (805/969-5046).

In April attend the Arts Festival (805/966-7022). The Santa Barbara Fiesta is held in early August, featuring music, dancing, a parade and many other festivities (Fiesta Office, 1122 Milpas Street, Santa Barbara, CA 93103; 805/962-8101) including a week-long horse show and rodeo at Earl Warren Showgrounds (805/969-4726).

102. Visit the Santa Barbara Mission and Archives, 2201 Laguna Street (805/682-4713).

Guided tours of El Presidio de Santa Barbara State Historic Park may be arranged by calling the park office (805/966-9719), located at 123 E. Canon Perdido. The park includes El Cuartel, a 1788 soldiers' quarters considered to be the second oldest building in California, the Padres' Quarters (a 15-minute slide show may be requested) and the authentically reconstructed and decorated Presidio Chapel.

Lunch on the terrace of El Encanto Hotel, 1900 Lasuen Road (805/687-5000), and in summer attend an afternoon concert presented by the Music Academy of the West (805/969-4726).

103. Roam through the Santa Barbara Botanical Gardens at 1212 Mission Canyon (805/682-4726) with its sixty-five acres of native California plants and walking trails, and stop at the Natural History Museum, 2559 Puesta del Sol Road in the same canyon (805/682-4711).

Visit the Historical Museum (136 E. De la Guerra Street; 805/966-1601) and the Karpeles Manuscript Museum (21 W. Anapumu; 805/962-5322) in downtown Santa Barbara. Also tour the Old Spanish Days Carriage Museum with its collection of more than seventy wagons, carts, coaches and carriages; note the mural by famed western artist Edward Borein (129 Castillo Street in Pershing Park; 805/962-2353).

Visit the Trusell-Winchester Adobe and the Victorian Fernald House, at 412 and 414 W. Montecito Street, which have been restored by the Santa Barbara Historical Society (P.O. Box 578, Santa Barbara, CA 93103).

104. Take the San Marcos Pass/Highway 154 to the Santa Ynez Valley (in spring the *ceanothus* is spectacularly in bloom), and take the Stagecoach Road loop on the valley side to see Cold Spring Tavern stage stop (805/967-0066) and the 1868 Road Gang House, with the tree growing through the eaves, which housed the Chinese builders of the road. Look up, and note the 700-foot Cold Spring Arch Bridge spanning the canyon 400 feet above.

Tour the Santa Ynez Valley Historical Society Museum & Parks-Janeway Carriage House at Sagunto and Faraday Streets in Santa Ynez (P.O. Box 181, Santa Ynez, CA 93460; 805/688-7889).

Lunch at historic Mattei's Tavern (805/688-4820; lunch weekends only), an 1886 stagecoach stop on Highway 154 in Los Olivos. You may wish to view art works at the Cody and some of the other local galleries. Or visit the Ballard Canyon (1825 Ballard Canyon Road), Firestone (Zaca Station Road near Foxen Canyon; 805/688-3940) and Zaca Mesa (Foxen Canyon Road) wineries.

Return south on Alamo Pintado Road, turning off on Baseline into Ballard, the valley's first settlement (1880). Stop at the 1889 Ballard Church (2465 Baseline; 805/688-6684) and the two-room 1882 Ballard School (Cottonwood & School Streets) still in use. Dine on French-American *haute cuisine* at The Ballard Store, 2449 Baseline (805/688-5319; the special vegetarian dinner "From the Garden" requires one day's notice.

105. From Santa Barbara, take Highway 101 north over Gaviota Pass; turn west on Highway 246 to Purisima Road, leading to La Purisima Mission State Historic Park (805/733-3713). The Mission fiesta is the third Sunday in May; call for information on other events.

Continue on three miles to Lompoc, and visit the Lompoc Museum at 200 S. H Street (Lompoc Historical Society, P.O. Box 88, Lompoc, CA 93438; 805/736-3888), which houses a collection of Chumash and other Indian artifacts in one of the nation's few remaining Carnegie Library buildings.

Have a traveler's supper: the famous split-pea soup at the original 1924 Andersen's in Buellton (Avenue of the Flags at Highway 246; 805/688-5581).

106. Visit the Danish settlement of Solvang in the Santa Ynez Valley, beginning with an *abelskiever* brunch. Stop at the Elverhoy Museum at 1624 Elverhoy Way (805/686-1211), housed in a typical 18th century Danish farm house. Visit the Bethania Lutheran Church at 603 Atterdag Road (805/688-4637); built in 1928, it is a fine example of 14th century Danish architecture. Investigate the shops: the Book Loft (1680 Mission Drive) has local history and natural history selections, Thumbelina (1685 Copenhagen Drive) has every color of DMC thread and an array of needlework kits and patterns, and other stores abound with Scandinavian imports. Tour Old Mission Santa Ines, founded in 1804. Have tea or coffee and assorted Danish pastries at Birkholm's (Alisal Road at Copenhagen Drive), which supplies these delicacies for SAS flights *to* Europe.

The Visitor's Information Center at 1660 Copenhagen Drive can provide maps of the town (805/688-1981). "Danish Days" in September celebrates the town's heritage with a parade, Danish foods, and entertainment (805/688-3317).

Ventura County

Friday, March 1, we came on to San Buenaventura, on the seacoast. Soon after leaving Cayeguas we entered the plain, which there lies along the sea, and crossed it to the sea about twenty miles. It is a fine grassy plain, with here and there a gentle green knoll, with a few dry creeks and alkaline ponds, and one fine stream, the Santa Clara River, running through it. . . . The houses are of adobe, the roofs of red tiles, and all dirty enough. A fine old church stands, the extensive garden now in ruins, but with a few palm trees and many figs and olives -- the old padres' garden.

Francis P. Farquhar, editor, *Up and Down California in 1860-1864: The Journal of William H. Brewer* (1930).

107. On Highway 126, note the historic marker at Rancho Camulos, where Helen Hunt Jackson gathered information on early California life for her novel *Ramona* (2.2 miles east of Piru). Continuing through the Santa Clara River Valley, pause to view the Piru Mansion in Piru (privately owned); following its tragic destruction by fire, the magnificent Victorian was painstakingly reconstructed using the original blueprints.

Also see Fillmore's Historical Museum, 4447 Main Street, housed in a former Southern Pacific railroad depot. The eclectic assortment of everyday objects combine to recreate the spirit of a small country community (Fillmore Historical Society, P.O. Box 314, Fillmore, CA 93015; 805/524-0948).

In Santa Paula visit Unocal's renovated and expanded California Oil Museum at Tenth and Main (805/525-6672), containing thirteen state-of-the-art exhibit areas. The *Queen Anne* building with its five-sided corner tower was erected in the 1880s to house the Santa Paula Hardware Company on the first floor, and the Hardison & Stewart Oil Company offices on the second; in 1890 the latter merged with the third floor Sespe & Torrey Canyon oil companies to form Union Oil Company of California, today's Unocal. Stop at the old Santa Paula Depot, Railroad Avenue and Tenth Street; the depot building now houses an art gallery and the city's Chamber of Commerce & Visitors' Bureau (805/525-5561). Lunch at the Glen

Tavern Inn, 134 N. Mill Street (call ahead, 805/525-6658 --
the Inn restaurant is occasionally restricted to resident
guests).

Return to Fillmore and turn south on County Road
23 to Highway 188, then east to visit Strathern Historical
Park, 137 Strathern Place off Madera Road in Simi Valley
(805/526-6453). Structures in the six-acre park include a
pre-1800 adobe, a turn-of-the-century farm house and two
large barns containing agricutural equipment, and the original one-room Simi Library.

108. On the way to Ventura visit the Stagecoach
Inn Museum, 51 S. Ventu Park Road in Newbury Park
(805/498-9441), where there is a collection of stagecoaches,
and other horsedrawn vehicles. There are also three village cultures portrayed in the park: Chumash Indian, Span-
ish/Mexican, and American pioneer.

Make a stop at the spacious two-story Olivas Adobe
and museum, 4200 Olivas Park Drive in Ventura (805/644-
4346), and drive along the 600 block of Mitchell Boulevard
with its eight vintage houses. Visit the Old Town Livery
at 34 N. Palm Street, a restored livery stable (ca. 1900),
with bookshop and a restaurant. Visit the 1857 Ortega
Adobe at 215 W. Main Street (805/648-5823). Proceed to
the 100 block of E. Main and the Buenaventura Mission
Plaza archaeological site and the Albinger Archaeological
Museum (805/648-5823). Tour the Ventura County Museum of History & Art, 100 E. Main Street; (805/653-0323)
and nearby Mission San Buenaventura (211 E. Main Street;
805/648-4496), and wander south down Main Street to investigate the many antique and "collectibles" shops. Stop
by the Old California Store, 1528 E. Thompson Boulevard,
and ask for their latest newsletter listing events of historical interest.

109. Visit the Port Hueneme Historical Museum,
located in an old bank building at Market and Hueneme
Roads in Port Hueneme. Then tour the Civil Engineer
Corps/SeaBee Museum on the Navy base, the second oldest
Navy museum in the country, and learn the history of the
Navy Construction Battalion (SeaBees). The collections are
extensive; this is one of the finest military museums in the
nation (Building 99, Naval Construction Battalion Center,
Channel Islands Boulevard and Ventura Road, Port Huen-
eme; 805/488-2023).

40

During Harbor Days in the Fall, you may tour Navy ships; there is also a parade, games and contests, foods, crafts, etc. (Port Hueneme Cultural Center: 805/488-2023).

110. Attend the Historic Waterfront Celebration in Ventura in October. There are tall ships at the State Pier, a railroad exhibit at the Fairgrounds and historical walking tours in the heart of town: entertainment, crafts, antique vehicles, etc. (805/654-7830).

111. Visit the Ojai Valley Museum, housed in an old fire station at 109 S. Montgomery Street in Ojai (805/646-2290). It contains objects from the culture of the 9000-year-old Oak Grove people and archaeological items of 3000-year-old Chumash Indian tribes, as well as more recent items of local historical interest. Ojai Realty (260 E. Ojai Avenue; 805/646-4331) provides a walking tour brochure of the city. Tours of the library are available at the Krotona Institute of Theosophy set in an 118-acre tree-filled estate (805/646-2653).

112. A Ventura County getaway could include a stop at the Ventura County Maritime Museum at Fisherman's Wharf, 2731 S. Victoria Avenue, Oxnard (805/486-9867).

In late September, include a visit to the Ventura Antiquarian Book Fair in Ventura. Contact the Ventura Visitors Bureau for specifics (805/654-7830).

113. Plan a day or a weekend on the Channel Islands. Island Packers (805/642-1393) books overnight guests into the rustic 100-year-old Scorpion Bay Ranch on Santa Cruz Island. Or, Channel Islands Adventure (805/987-1678) will take you to the Christy Ranch in the island's interior.

II. TOPICAL TOURS

Antiques

Inside the monastery, life was simple and comfortless. The floors were earthen or tiled; there were few fireplaces, and the windows were glassless. The furnishings consisted of plain, straight, oak chairs with rawhide seats and backs or straight, hard benches, hand-hewn and without paint or decoration. The refectory table was heavy, long and plain.

Mackey and Sooy, *Early California Costumes* (1932).

114. Attend a western antique appraisal session at Glendora's Orange Tree Bazaar, 216 N. Glendora Avenue, with its 40 shops, followed by box lunches at the Martin House, headquarters of the San Dimas Historical Society (246 E. Bonita Avenue; 714/592-1190).

Spend the afternoon browsing through some of the 400 shops of Pomona's Antique Row -- the 100 and 200 blocks of E. Second Street (1-800-794-0344) -- including Robbin's Antiques (714/983-9548).

Or wander through Ontario's 14,000-square-foot Antique Underground.

115. Study restoration techniques at the Architectural-Crafts Fair held each April at the Workman & Temple Family Homestead Museum, 15415 E. Don Julian Road in the City of Industry (818/968-8492).

Other restoration workshops are conducted by Heritage Square Museum (818/449-0193) and Pasadena Heritage (818/793-0617).

116. Visit the Center for the Study of Decorative Arts, and arrange for a presentation on California decorative traditions (31431 Camino Capistrano, San Juan Capistrano, CA 92675; 714/496-2131).

117. On a specially arranged tour, study the techniques of making Tiffany-style glass at the Judson Studios, 220 S. Avenue 66 in Los Angeles (213/255-0131). Observe painstaking restoration at nearby Heritage

Square, 3800 Homer off Avenue 43 (818/796-2898), inviting a Heritage Square restoration specialist to comment. Other restoration experts are available at the Banning Residence Museum (310/548-7777), or at the Workman Temple Homestead (818/968-8492).

Notes

Architecture

Los Angeles is instant architecture in an instant townscape. Most of its buildings are the first and only structures on their particular parcels of land; they are couched in a dozen different styles, most of them imported, exploited, and ruined within living memory. Yet the city has a comprehensible, even consistent, quality to its built form, unified enough to rank as a fit subject for an historical monograph.

Reyner Banham, *Los Angeles: The Architecture of Four Ecologies* (1984).

118. Learn about the creation of the J. Paul Getty Museum, 17985 Pacific Coast Highway (310/458-2003), modeled on the Villa de Papyri. Arrange with the museum staff for a discussion on the construction of this historical replica.

119. Review a mission restoration. View the exterior of earthquake-damaged Mission San Gabriel Archangel (537 W. Mission Drive in San Gabriel), followed by a slide lecture on the subject.

Lunch at Lawry's California Center at 370 W. Avenue 26, Los Angeles (213/224-6850).

Continue on to Mission San Fernando Rey de Espana (15151 San Fernando Mission Boulevard in Mission Hills; 818/365-1501), completely reconstructed after the 1971 Sylmar earthquake.

120. Take a docent-led tour of the 1908 Greene and Greene masterpiece Gamble House and gardens, 4 Westmorland, parallel to the 300 block of N. Orange Grove (818/793-3334). Follow the neighborhood walking guide, available at the Gamble House bookstore. Venture along Pasadena's Arroyo Boulevard, into the *Craftsman* Bohemia of the lower Arroyo homes of Olive Percival, Charles Lummis, etc.

121. Inspect Southern California tilework at the 1929 *Moorish-Spanish Colonial Revival* Rhonda Adamson Home at Malibu Lagoon State Park, 23200 Pacific Coast Highway (310/456-8432). The Malibu Lagoon Museum adjoins the home. Directly across the highway, proceed carefully up the hill to the Serra Retreat House at 34015 Serra Road. It incorporates tile used in the Rindge estate, former occupant of the site (P.O. Box 127, Malibu, CA 90265; 310/456-6631). May Rindge was a pioneer settler who, by opposing construction of the Southern Pacific Railroad, made this property the most sought after single real estate holding in the U.S. Note the famed Malibu Pier, once owned by Rindge; she opposed the pier's use for off-loading of railroad materials.

Follow with a seaside luncheon at the Sand Castle on the beach in Malibu, or at Alice's Restaurant (23000 Pacific Coast Highway; 310/456-6646). Make a return trip stop at the Santa Monica Heritage Museum, 2612 Main Street in Santa Monica (310/392-8537).

122. Take a walking tour of the *Moderne* and *International Style* (modern) architecture in the Silverlake district, including the Kesling houses on Easterly Terrace and the Neutra houses on nearby Silverwood Terrace and Silverlake Drive, with a possible visit to Neutra's final home, now owned by Cal Poly Pomona (School of Environmental Design: 714/869-2666). Follow with a short drive to Micheltorena Avenue, the location of buildings by Arnold Schindler, Gregory Ain and John Lautner, as well as the home of the celebrated evangelist Aimee Semple McPherson. Consult Gebhard & Winter, *Architecture in Los Angeles: A Compleat Guide*, pp. 183-188.

Lunch at La Nikola, 4326 W. Sunset Boulevard (213/660-7217).

123. Explore innovative Southern California architecture with views of the *Art Moderne* St. James Club at 8358 W. Sunset, the nearby *International* Schindler house at 833 N. Kings Road, and the virtually unaltered 1935 *Streamline Moderne* Gilmore Gasoline Service Station at 859 N. Highland Avenue near Melrose; visit the *Post Moderne* Pacific Design Center at 8687 Melrose. Lunch at the Hotel Mondrian, 8440 W. Sunset Boulevard (213/650-8999); its exterior is decorated in the style made famous by Dutch *Modernist* Piet Mondrian.

124. Study the range of Wallace Neff's architectural contributions in a presentation at El Molino Viejo, 1120 Old Mill Road, San Marino (California Historical So ciety: 818/449-5450). Follow with a visit to selected Neff houses including 1883 and 2115 Orlando Road in San Marino and Alverno High School, 200 N. Michillinda Avenue in Sierra Madre, a Tuscan villa designed by Neff in 1925. For a speaker, contact the American Institute of Architects, 8687 Melrose Avenue, Los Angeles, CA 90069 (310/659-2282).

125. Mark Black History Month with the American Institute of Architects' slide show on Paul R. Williams (213/380-4595) and visits to Beverly Hills buildings designed by Williams, including Saks Fifth Avenue at 9600 Wilshire Boulevard, Litton Industries at 360 N. Crescent Drive and several stars' homes. Consult the Beverly Hills Historic Resources Survey prepared by Johnson & Associates, available at the Beverly Hills Public Library, 444 N. Rexford Drive (310/288-2244). Williams' own home stands at 1690 Victoria Avenue on Lafayette Square in Los Angeles.

126. With the assistance of a speaker from the UCLA Interior & Environmental Design Program, explore *California ranch house* architecture developed in the postwar years by Southern California architect Cliff May. With the help of the American Institute of Architects (3780 Wilshire Boulevard, Los Angeles, CA 90010; 213/380-4595) try to arrange a visit to "Mandalay," his quintessential ranch house on Old Ranch Road in Sullivan Canyon. Also visit some of his many houses in nearby Riviera Ranch and Old Oak in Pacific Palisades. Consult Gebhard & Winter, *Architecture in Los Angeles: A Compleat Guide*, p. 120.

127. Study the architecture of Quincy Jones in a slide presentation developed by the USC architectural faculty. Follow with a visit to his last home, a 1965 conversion of a large wood-clad photography studio aptly named "the Barn," at 10300 Little Santa Monica Boulevard near Century City (USC Architectural Guild: 310/470-6066).

Or visit CSU Dominguez Hills, for which Jones was a master planner (310/516-3300).

128. Examine L.A.'s eclectic church architecture including Church of the Angels at 1100 N. Avenue 64 in Highland Park (*Cotswold Gothic*), St. Andrew's (*Romanes-*

que) and Lake Avenue Congregational (*Contemporary*) in Pasadena, Wee Kirk o' the Heather at Forest Lawn in Glendale, Our Lady Queen of Angels at the Plaza (modified *Spanish Colonial*), St. Vincent's at Adams and Figueroa (*Churigueresque*) and neighboring St. John's Episcopal at 514 W. Adams (*Italian Romanesque*; an exact copy of the Church of San Miniato in Florence, Italy), the Second Church of Christ Scientist at 948 W. Adams Boulevard (*Greek Revival*) St. Sophia's Greek Orthodox Cathedral at 1324 S. Normandie Avenue (*Byzantine*), First Congregational at 6th and Commonwealth (*Gothic*), Wilshire Boulevard Temple at 3663 Wilshire & Hobart (modified *Byzantine*), and St. Basil's at Wilshire & Kingsley (*Coventry Modern*). Lunch in the garden of the Sheraton Townhouse at 2961 Wilshire Boulevard (213/382-7171).

A San Gabriel Valley church of note is St. John the Baptist Catholic Church in Baldwin Park (3843 Baldwin Park Boulevard; 818/960-2795). It was completely redecorated in 1983 by designer Tony Duquette.

129. As guests of Altadena Heritage (P.O. Box 218, Altadena, CA 91003: 818/798-1268) take a driving tour of old Altadena, past the 1890 Gillette Hunting Lodge at 1391 E. Palm Street, Zane Grey's house, designed by Myron Hunt, at 396 Lake Avenue, the Woodbury house (c. 1882), and the McNally house (c. 1887) as well as several Greene & Greenes, a Frank Lloyd Wright, a Neutra, a Myron Hunt and a 1958 Case Study house by the firm of Buff Straub & Hensman.

130. Take one of the several architectural walking tours offered by the Los Angeles Conservancy: "Terra Cotta," "Art Deco" or "Marble Masterpieces." Call 213/623-CITY for individual or group reservations.

Take a drive around the park -- Los Angeles' MacArthur Park (Los Angeles Historic-Cultural Monument No. 100), established in 1887 as Westlake Park and now location of construction for the Metro Red Line subway -- to view the once luxury hotels and apartments of the 1920s: the Asbury Hotel Apartments, and the Arcady, Ansonia, Bryson, Leighton, Olympia and Parkway Hotels. The Westlake Theatre facade also dates from the period.

Bertram Goodhue's 1924 Elks Building, now the Park Plaza Hotel (607 S. Park View) reflects proto-*Art Deco* influences; you may view the interiors painted by Anthony

Heinsbergen. Lunch at nearby La Fonda restaurant, Los Angeles Historic-Cultural Monument No. 268 (2501 Wilshire Boulevard; 213/380-5055).

131. View examples of Frank Lloyd Wright's architecture in the Hollywood area with a guided tour of Hollyhock House, built for millionaire oil heiress Aline Barnsdall (Barnsdall Art Park, 4808 Hollywood Boulevard; 213/662-7272). Arrange for a guided tour of the Ennis House at 2607 Glendower Avenue, and of the Storer House at 8161 Hollywood Boulevard, as guests of the USC School of Architecture (213/740-2723).

132. Take an architectural tour of San Diego County with stops in La Jolla at Louis Kahn's *Modernist* Salk Institute (10010 N. Torrey Pines Boulevard: 619/453-4100) and Irving Gill's Bishop's School (7607 La Jolla Boulevard: 619/459-4021), La Jolla Women's Club (715 Silverado at Prospect: 619/454-2354), and Museum of Contemporary Art (700 Prospect: 619/454-3541). Lunch at La Jolla's historic La Valencia Hotel (1132 Prospect: 619/454-0771), landscaped by prominent horticulturist Kate Sessions.

View three *Post Modern* architectural complexes: The Aventine Plaza, 8910 University Center Lane, San Diego (619/597-2400), the Horton Plaza at 4th & Broadway in downtown San Diego (619/238-1596), and Michael Graves' San Juan Capistrano Public Library, 31495 El Camino Real (714/493-3984).

Art

The impressionistic style practiced by Los Angeles artists was not a rote copy of European or Eastern American styles, but a particularly distinct local form, shaped by local climatic and geological characteristics. The dry terrain -- most often characterized by golden grasses, dusky green bushes, and the rose, ochres and grays of dormant or dry foliage -- set painters' color schemes in an earthy range of ochres, tans, and pale greens. Because distant landscape features without the benefit of atmospheric perspective appear closer than they are, Southern California painters often stacked landscape elements on the canvas as decorative shapes rather than cause them to recede into a three-dimensional composition. In addition, Southern California's bolder, more rugged forms -- the exposed rocky silhouettes of mountains, the naked molded contours of the hills, its dark green gnarled oaks, giant granite boulders, and heavy brush, as opposed to the more heavily foliated East -- made California landscapes more rugged, less sweet, than Eastern works.

Nancy W. Moure, *Painting and Sculpture in Los Angeles, 1900-1945* (1980).

133. Learn about the "plaine air painters" in a discussion and exhibit of Southern California's turn-of-the-century watercolorists, presented at the Virginia Steele Scott Gallery of the Huntington Library, 1151 Oxford Road, San Marino (818/405-2100).

134. Take an art tour of the UCLA campus, including the Franklin D. Murphy Sculpture Gardens and the Frederick S. Wight Gallery in the Dickson Art Center (UCLA Visitors' Center: 310/825-3264).

Continue the tour at the Armand Hammer Museum, 10889 Wilshire Boulevard (310/443-7000).

135. Attend the Festival of Folk Art held each May at the L.A. County Museum of Natural History in Exposition Park (213/744-3466).

136. Explore indigenous folk art with a guided tour of the Watts Towers of Simon Rodia State Historic

Park at 1765 E. 107th Street (213/569-8181), and in the adjoining South Gallery view the permanent installation of a folk instrument exhibit from around the world.

Visit St. Elmo's Village in the 4800 block of St. Elmo Drive (213/935-6123) and the Craft & Folk Art Museum at 5814 Wilshire Boulevard (213/937-5544).

137. BIG art: take an astonishing art tour of the freeway murals and artists' lofts in downtown L.A. The tour could include visits to billboard centers: Foster & Kleiser (213/731-5111) and Pacific Outdoor Advertising (213/222-7171). Visit MOCA (Museum of Contemporary Art) at the Temporary Contemporary, 152 N. Central Avenue (213/626-6222), and lunch at Gorkey's Cafe, 536 E. 8th (213/627-4060).

138. View examples of outdoor art and sculpture in downtown Los Angeles, beginning with Claus Oldenburg's "Ladder" at Loyola Law School, 1441 W. Olympic Boulevard (213/736-1000). Visit the Mayan Theatre with its brightly painted sculptured facade, at 1040 S. Hill Street. At the Jewelry Mart at 6th and Hill Streets, view Michael Hayden's 270-foot-long "Generators of the Cylinder;" its neon tubes, which flash in successive circles, are powered by viewers' body heat. Visit the Fine Arts Building (811 W. 7th Street), its exterior an exact replica of Or' San Michele in Lucca, Italy, and its two-story lobby a genuine *tour-de-force* accented with Ernest Bachelder tiles. Immediately to the west is the richly embellished *Beaux Arts* Home Savings & Loan office at 7th and Figueroa Streets.

Visit MOCA, the Museum of Contemporary Art, at 250 S. Grand Avenue (213/62-MOCA-2). Take a picnic lunch to a noon concert, held in the adjacent California Plaza Spiral Court on Wednesdays and Fridays throughout the summer (300 S. Grand Avenue; 213/687-2159).

View Herbert Bayer's fountain sculpture, "Double Ascension," in the courtyard of Atlantic Richfield Plaza, Flower Street between 5th and 6th Streets, and cross to the northeast corner of Flower and 5th to an outdoor courtyard displaying works by Robert Rauschenberg, Frank Stella and Mark Suvero. Proceed up the stairway connecting 5th and Hope Streets. View "Mind, Body and Spirit" by Gidon Graetz in front of the Stu Ketchum YMCA at 4th and Hope Streets; on the opposite corner you will find

Alexander Liberman's "Ulysses". Cross the courtyard and enter the O'Melveny and Meyers Building at 400 S. Hope Street to tour the changing art exhibits assembled by this 100-year-old Los Angeles law firm. Proceed to the Security Pacific Plaza to view the red steel-arched Alexander Calder stabile, and tour the changing exhibits at the Plaza level exhibition gallery (333 S. Hope; 213/345-5555). Cross the street to the Wells Fargo Center, 333 S. Grand Avenue (213/253-4200), to view Louise Nevelson's massive sculpture, "Night Sail" in the courtyard and Jean Miro's 1967 sculpture "Le Caressa de Oiseau" in the lobby, as well as works by Jean Debuffet, Robert Graham and Nancy Graves.

Dinner by the windows at Steps on the Court (330 S. Hope; 213/626-0900) on weeknights will provide an unstaged demonstration of performance art, as cyclists work out on the glass-walled second floor of the YMCA building.

139. A look at Latino mural art could begin with a visit to the Italian Hall in El Pueblo Historic Monument (213/680-2525) for observation of the painstaking preservation techniques being used on the Sequeiros mural, "Tropical America". Include the many murals to be found around the 3000 block of E. Olympic Boulevard in Boyle Heights; consult *Map Guide to the Murals of Los Angeles* (Los Angeles Mural Conservancy: 310/854-0146).

For more Latino art, follow with a visit to Self-Help-Graphics, an art co-op at 3802 Brooklyn Avenue in East L.A. (213/264-1259).

140. Explore Santa Monica's public art -- from its 1938 WPA murals to contemporary expressions and innovations -- with a self-guided walking tour. *Guide to Public Art in Santa Monica* is obtainable at the visitors' center, 1400 Ocean Avenue in Palisades Park, or from the Department of Cultural & Recreation Services, Santa Monica City Hall Rm. 210, 1685 Main Street.

141. Take an art tour of Costa Mesa in Orange County, beginning with a docent-led tour of the Orange County Performing Arts Center at Town Center Drive (714/556-2787). Cross the San Diego Freeway to South Coast Plaza Town Center at 3333 Bristol Street (714/241-1700) to view the impressive sculptural installation created by the late Isamu Noguchi entitled "California Scenario." Visit the nearby Security Pacific Bank Gallery at 555 Anton Boulevard (714/433-6290).

Lunch at the art-filled Meridian Hotel, 4500 MacArthur Boulevard, Newport Beach (714/476-2001). Lahaina Galleries will provide a guided tour of the art collection (714/721-9117).

142. Witness transient art at one of the sand castle contests held on southland beaches: Santa Barbara (805/966-6110) in June; San Clemente (714/492-4036) and San Diego's U.S. Open (619/424-6663) in July; Santa Monica (213/380-4595), Manhatten Beach (310/546-8857) and Redondo Beach (310/318-0630) in August; or Seal Beach (714/660-7600) and Corona del Mar (Orange County Sandcastle Competition 714/557-7796, and Newport SeaFest 714/644-8211) in September. You can see artists at work in the morning; judging takes place in the afternoon.

143. Take a nocturnal neon tour via double-decker bus through downtown Los Angeles, West L.A. and the San Fernando Valley with the Museum of Neon Art (704 Traction Avenue: 213/617-1580) to see the city illuminated with vivid neon signs used in the early part of the century for the first time in the United States by Earl C. Anthony of Los Angeles.

144. Pay a visit to Grandma Prisbrey's Bottle Village, 4595 Cochran Street, Simi Valley. In 1956 Tressa Prisbrey began creating a fanciful village from a variety of recycled materials. The resulting folk art environment includes thirteen buildings and twenty sculptures.

Athletics and Sports

The Olympic committee in Los Angeles erected a village for the athletes on Angelus Mesa -- the old Baldwin ranch. Water of the exact chemical properties of their drinking water at home was provided for each team -- also native cooks for each country. In front of each working sportswriter in the press stand was a stock ticker, continuously printing out results and figures -- not only at the track in front of his eyes, but at other places where boat races, horsemanship events, fencing matches were going on. The tracks were lightning fast; they were of peat -- impossible in any country where rains are uncertain.

Harry Carr, Los Angeles: City of Dreams (1935).

145. Visit the First Interstate Bank Athletic Foundation Museum at 2141 West Adams (213/614-4111), formerly the Britt mansion (1909). Follow with a guided tour of the Los Angeles Coliseum, 3911 S. Figueroa Street (213/747-7111).

Stop to see the 1923 *Spanish Colonial* headquarters of the Automobile Club of Southern California at 2601 S. Figueroa Street (213/741-3111). The rotunda's golden dome and its elaborate tile ornamentation are worth a brief visit.

146. "Take Me Out to the Ball Game!" Arrange for a presentation on the Dodgers' move to Los Angeles, along with a reception and a buffet dinner at the waterfall gardens of the L.A. Police Academy, 1880 N. Academy Drive (213/221-3101). Follow with a short walk to Dodger Stadium and a night game of the Angels/Dodgers Freeway Series.

147. Take a gallop through Southern California history at the Santa Anita Horse Museum & Library at the California Racing Hall of Fame, 201 Colorado Place, Arcadia (818/446-8512).

During racing season you may breakfast and watch the horses being exercised on the track (enter via Gate 8), and on weekends take a guided tram tour of the stables (Santa Anita Race Track, 205 W. Huntington Drive: (818/574-7223).

148. Visit the Ralph W. Miller Memorial Golf Library and museum at the Industry Hills & Sheraton Resort on the hill above Azusa Avenue, City of Industry (818/965-0861), for a presentation on the history of California golf. See the replica of St. Andrew's Golf Course Railway Station in Scotland, where golf began; parked on the siding is Winston Churchill's funeral car.

149. Tour the Museum of Roger Penski Racing Cars located at Longo Toyota, 3534 N. Peck Road, El Monte (818/580-6000). Ride around the town on one of the city buses, replicas of old trolley cars.

Or attend the Toyota Grand Prix, held each April on the streets of downtown Long Beach, to see racing cars in action (310/436-9953).

150. Visit some of the Pasadena sites where Jackie Robinson developed his skill in baseball. Robinson was the first African-American to break the color barrier in major league baseball; after baseball, he promoted goodwill and educational excellence. His old alma mater, Grover Cleveland Elementary School, is located at 524 Palisade Street; a community center which bears his name is at 1020 N. Fair Oaks. The program could include a showing of the movie *The Jackie Robinson Story*, perhaps at the restored Pasadena Central Library, 285 E. Walnut Street (818/405-4607). Consult the California Afro-American Museum (213/744-7432) or the Altadena Historical Society (P.O. Box 144, Altadena, CA 91001) for background information.

151. Visit the Huntington Beach International Surfing Museum, which commemorates the sport and culture of surfing (411 Olive Avenue, Huntington Beach; 714/960-3483). In July the International Surf Festival rotates between Huntington Beach, Redondo Beach, Torrance, Hermosa Beach, and Manhattan Beach (310/545-4502).

Business

"I am a foresighted man, I believe that Los Angeles is destined to become the most important city in this country, if not in the world. It can extend in any direction as far as you like; its front door opens on the Pacific, the ocean of the future. The Atlantic is the ocean of the past. Europe can supply her own wants; we shall supply the wants of Asia. There is nothing that cannot be made and few things that will not grow in Southern California. It has the finest climate in the world: extremes of heat and cold are unknown. These are the reasons for its growth."

Henry E. Huntington as quoted by A. Edward Newton in "The Course of Empire," *The Atlantic Monthly* (March, 1932).

152. Take one of the following L.A. Conservancy tours (213/623-CITY):

"Palaces of Finance"   "Union Station"
"Broadway Theatres"   "Mecca for Merchants"
                         "Pershing Square Landmarks"
Stop at Philippe "the Original" Restaurant (1924) at 1001 N. Alameda (213/628-3781) for the justly famous French-dip sandwiches.

153. Entrepreneurs of the Inland Empire: visit the 1894 Graber Olive House at 315 E. 4th Street in Ontario (714/983-1761), and the permanent GE Hotpoint exhibit, documenting its development in the area, at the Ontario Museum of History and Art, 255 Euclid (714/983-3198). Tour the former Guasti Mansion & Winery, once known as the world's largest winery, at 2903 E. Guasti Road (714/983-5512). Lunch in the historic diner directly north of the Guasti Mansion.

Arrange with a professor of history from Cal Poly, Pomona (714/629-2301), or with the local historical society, for a visit to Richard Gird's historic sugar beet mill, 5165 G Street in Chino, the largest one in the U.S. when it was built in the 1890s. Request a presentation about Gird at the Old Schoolhouse Museum (Chino Historical Society: 714/628-1950).

154. Follow the steps of Californians who changed the national breakfast: begin with brunch at Kellogg Hall, winter home of cornflake developer W.W. Kellogg, on the campus of Cal Poly Pomona, 3801 W. Temple (714/869-3860). Visit the Pomona Public Library, where the Special Collections Department has an extensive collection of colorful packing-crate labels.

This could be followed by a visit to the Weber House and orange grove, located in the 4800 block of Via de Mansion in La Verne, as guests of the La Verne Heritage Foundation (714/596-7894, 596-8726).

Proceed to Riverside where one of California's original Washington Navel orange trees still thrives. In 1873, two greenhouse grown trees were sent to Mrs. Eliza Tibbets. Bud stock taken from her trees made the region the leading navel orange producer in the world. Tour beautifully restored Heritage House, 8193 Magnolia Avenue (714/689-1333). For speakers contact the history departments at Cal Poly Pomona (714/869-3860) and/or UC Riverside (714/787-1012). You might also contact the Orange County Citrus Historical Society, 18621 Lassen Drive, Santa Ana, CA 92705.

155. An Excursion in Economics: visit the Wells Fargo History Museum at 3rd & Grand (213/253-7166), the museum in the Federal Reserve Bank of San Francisco at 9th & Grand (213/683-2300) and the Mark Taper Hall of Economics and Finance in the California Museum of Science and Industry, Exposition Park (213/744-7400).

Invite a speaker to tell the story of Los Angeles' early Farmers & Merchants Bank, which later evolved into the Security Pacific National Bank.

156. A.M. in L.A. -- join The Next Stage (213/934-2216) or Round Town Tours (310/836-7559) for an early morning visit to the Flower Mart at 755 S. Wall Street (213/627-2482), as described in historian David Clark's *L.A. on Foot*. Breakfast at Vickman's, 1228 E. 8th (213/622-3852), a Los Angeles tradition since 1919, and explore the garment district.

157. Take a guided tour of the *Los Angeles Times* Olympic Plant, 200 E. 8th Street (213/237-5000). Follow with a rib-sticking lunch at the Pantry, a Los Angeles institution since 1924 (877 S. Figueroa at 8th Street: 213/972-9279).

158. Doing Business in Old Los Angeles: visit some of L.A.'s century-old businesses: Wolcott's Stationers (1893) at 214 W. Spring, Darling's Flowers (1895) at 1217 W. Temple, Fowler's Book Store (1888) at 717 W. 7th, Bekins Moving & Storage (1891) at 5461 W. Jefferson Boulevard, Ralph's Grocery Store at 3456 W. 3rd Street and Robinson's (1883) at 600 W. 7th.

159. May is "Water Month." Contact the Metropolitan Water District speakers' bureau (213/250-6485) for an illustrated lecture describing the construction of the impressive Colorado River Aqueduct. Arrange for a tour of the Weymouth filtration plant near Foothill Boulevard and Damien Avenue, La Verne.

160. Start with a visit to the *zanja* exhibit in the Avila Adobe on Olvera Street (El Pueblo de Los Angeles Historic Monument: 213/680-2525). Then tour the museum exhibits on the first floor of the Department of Water & Power, 111 N. Hope at Temple. Lunch in the cafeteria of the Water & Power building. Contact the Historical Society of Southern California for a speaker on the history of the Los Angeles Aqueduct (213/222-0546).

161. Learn about early oil exploration in California by visiting the West Kern Oil Museum at Highway 33 and Wood Street in Taft, which has the original 1917 wooden derrick over the original well, along with three acres of exhibits -- including a replica of Sutter's Fort -- where the history of Kern County oil exploration is traced (P.O. Box 491, Taft, CA 93266).

162. Honor Southern California's multi-ethnic tradition of coastal fishing by attending the annual Fishermen's Fiesta in San Pedro on the first weekend of October (Fishermen's Wharf, 22nd and Signal Streets, San Pedro). In addition to the blessing of the fleet, witness nettying contests, etc. For more information call the San Pedro Chamber of Commerce, 310/832-7272.
Follow with a visit to the Los Angeles Maritime Museum, Berth 84 at the foot of 6th Street (310/548-7618), and dinner at nearby Nizetich's in Ports O' Call at 1050

Nagoya Street (310/514-3878). Consult the San Pedro Bay Historical Society (310/548-3208) concerning a possible speaker.

Notes

Ethnic: People, Places & Celebrations

The east side of Los Angeles has always been the area of first settlement for immigrant groups in Southern California: Russians, Armenians, Russian-Armenians, Poles, Mexicans and Jews, particularly Russian-Jewish groups. As late as 1880, Boyle Heights, on the east side, was a fashionable residential district, but, particularly after 1908, it began to be taken over by immigrant groups. It is, in effect, an incubator which retains the immigrant groups until the influence of the first generation has begun to decline and the second generation has matured.

Carey McWilliams, *Southern California: An Island on the Land* (1946).

163. Take a walking tour of El Pueblo Historic Park taking special note of the Chinese, French, Italian and Latino influences on the history of Los Angeles (213/680-2525). Follow with a visit to the former French Hospital founded in the 1860s, now the Pacific Alliance Medical Center (College and Hill Streets), and to the Chinese-language public library at College and Yale Streets.

164. Take a guided walking tour of Little Tokyo sponsored by the Japanese Cultural Community Center, 244 S. San Pedro Street (213/620-0570), or with the Los Angeles Conservancy (213/623-CITY).

165. Explore the culture of Finland with a visit to the Finnish Folk Art Museum in the gardens of the Pasadena Historical Museum, 470 W. Walnut Street at Orange Grove (818/577-1660). The museum is a replica of a peasant home of the Province of Ostrobothnia in western Finland, containing a large living room (*tupa*) with an open hearth to serve both as cooking stove and fireplace. Traditional and typical furnishings date from the 17th to the 19th centuries, including hand carved wedding chairs, painted chests, birch bark utensils, double-decker beds (*ylisanky* or *kokkasanky*), and rag rugs (*rasymatto*).

166. Plan an all-day tour of L.A.'s Jewish History by chartered bus, presented by the Jewish Historical Society of Southern California (6505 Wilshire Boulevard, Los Angeles; 213/653-7740).

167. Visit the Martyrs Memorial & Museum of the Holocaust, depicting the 1933-1945 history of European Jews (6501 Wilshire Boulevard, Los Angeles; 213/651-3175).

Tour the Skirball Museum on the campus of Hebrew Union College (32nd and Hoover Streets, Los Angeles; 213/749-3424). Note: the College and Museum are moving to a new location sometime in 1992.

Another museum, scheduled to open in April of 1992, is the Beit Hashoah Museum of Tolerance at 9786 W. Pico Boulevard.

168. Take a walking tour of Chinatown under the guidance of the Chinese Historical Society of Southern California (978 N. Broadway, Los Angeles, CA 90012; 213/626-5240). The Society also publishes a walking tour map (see Self-Guided Tours, Appendix A).

Afterwards, you may wish to visit the historic 1888 Chinese Cemetery Shrine, which includes an altar and two ceremonial burners, at the east end of Evergreen Cemetery, 204 N. Evergreen Avenue in Boyle Heights.

169. Explore Latino traditions then and now with visits to the Juan Matias Sanchez Adobe, 946 Adobe Avenue, Montebello (213/887-4592), and to the historical museum in Garvey Ranch Park, 731 S. Orange, Monterey Park (City Administration: 818/307-1255), curated by the Historical Society of Monterey Park. Follow with a visit to El Mercado at 3425 E. 1st Street, Los Angeles, with its produce displays, food stalls and mariachi music. A option for lunch is Tamayo's, 5300 Olympic Boulevard at Atlantic, distinguished by the large mural executed by Rufino Tamayo.

170. Attend an Hungarian-Transylvanian village-style dance party with refreshments at Hungarian House, 1975 W. Washington Boulevard (213/737-8973).

171. Tour the Hsi Lai Buddhist Temple at 3456 S. Glenmark Drive in Hacienda Heights (818/961-9697), where the main shrine is dominated by three gilded Buddhas and hung with golden chandeliers, and hundreds of small Buddha figures sit in wall niches.

172. Spend a festive night in Belgrade -- meet Southern California's Yugoslav community and enjoy memorable Serbian cuisine at St. Steven's Social Center, 2511 W. Garvey Avenue, Alhambra (818/284-9100, or 714/629-2301).

173. Enjoy story-telling and dance at the African Marketplace, held the third weekend of each month at the William Grant Still Community Arts Center, 2520 West View, one block east of La Brea (213/734-1164).

Twenty-three African cultures are brought together at the African Marketplace and Cultural Faire held in Rancho Cienega Park in August (5001 Rodeo Boulevard, Los Angeles; 213/237-1540).

174. In February, celebrate the Chinese New Year in cooperation with the Chinese Historical Society (310/828-6911).

175. Celebrate Black History Month in February with a guided tour by Our Authors Study Club (213/295-0521) or by the History & Education Council of the California Afro-American Museum (213/744-7432). Include a tour of the California Afro-American Museum in Exposition Park, Los Angeles.

The Golden State Mutual Life Insurance Company building houses two large murals portraying the history of Blacks in California, and contains an Afro-American art collection (1999 W. Adams Boulevard; 213/731-1131 x237). Visit Biddy Mason Park, dedicated to a former slave who became a major Los Angeles land owner and philanthropist (333 S. Spring Street).

Pasadena Historical Society's video on Blacks in Southern California may also be available (818/577-1660).

176. Mark the St. Joseph's Day festivities on March 19 with a visit to St. Joseph's Table at St. Peter's Italian Church in the 1000 block of N. Broadway (213/225-8119, 226-9018) followed by lunch and tour at the nearby San Antonio Winery, 737 Lamar Street (213/223-1401).

177. In Spring, celebrate the festive East Indian holiday of *Sri Rama Navant* by visiting the Svee Venkataswaru Temple, located on more than four acres in the Malibu hills off Malibu Canyon Road, which has been constructed according to Hindu guidelines laid out in the 10th century. The visit could be followed by a stop at the ten-acre Self-Realization Fellowship Lake Shrine at 17190 Sunset Boulevard in Pacific Palisades (310/454-4114). Dine at the Dhabu India Restaurant at 2104 Main Street in Santa Monica, or at Sheesh Mahal at 5947 W. Pico Boulevard (213/936-2050).

178. In early April mark Buddha's birthday with *Hanamatsuri* festivities, which include processions through Little Tokyo, flower-arranging demonstrations and the traditional tea ceremony at the Japanese American Cultural Center (213/628-2725), and commemorative services in local Buddhist temples including the Los Angeles Hompa Honwanji Buddhist Temple at 815 E. 1st Street (213/680-9130).

179. On the weekend before April 13, celebrate the traditional Thai new year of *Songkran* at the Wat Thai Theravada Buddhist Center at 12909 Cantara Street, North Hollywood (818/997-9657), by attending morning services at the Wat Thai Temple followed by a carnival. Request comments by a member of the Asian American Studies Center, UCLA (213/825-2974).

180. In April, join in the celebration of *Kodomo-no-hi*, Children's Day, featuring games, and Asian arts and crafts, at the Japanese Cultural Community Center, 244 S. San Pedro Street (213/628-2725).

181. The Scandinavian Heritage Festival is held each April on the campus of California Lutheran University, 60 W. Olsen Road, Thousand Oaks (805/493-3151). There are arts and crafts, folk dancing, music and great food!

182. In April, the Imperial Valley Swiss community in Holtville holds their "Swiss Sing" and an exciting Swiss-style wrestling competition (619/356-2923). In October, the Octoberfest/Schwingfest includes traditional dancing and a bratwurst dinner. The Swiss Museum will be open.

183. In May, there are bagpipe bands and athletic events such as hammer-throw and tossing the *caber* at the

Scottish Highland Games held at the Orange County Fairgrounds (Fair Drive off Fairview Road south from the San Diego Freeway 405 in Costa Mesa; 714/751-3247).

184. In May, plan to attend the Pacific Islander Festival honoring the traditions of Hawaii, Samoa, Tonga, Guam, the Marshall Islands, the Maori of New Zealand and the Maohi of French Polynesia (Harbor Regional Park; 213/485-6759).

185. Attend the Grand National Irish Fair & Music Festival in early June (310/202-8846), followed by a visit to Des Regan's Irish Pub, 4311 W. Magnolia in Burbank (818/845-1036).

186. Mark the *Obon* Festival, a Japanese celebration occurring in June and July, which is devoted to the remembrance of ancestors. The Higashi Honganji Buddhist Temple at 505 E. 3rd Street (213/626-4200) stages many activities, including *bon odori*, the traditional *Obon* dance, as well as drum and dance performances, art exhibits and sushi bar.

The Gardena Valley Japanese Institute also stages an *Obon* parade (16215 S. Gramercy Place, Gardena, CA 90247; 213/770-2878).

The East San Gabriel Valley Japanese Community Center, 1203 W. Puente Avenue in West Covina, invites the public to its annual *Obon* Festival (818/337-9123, 960-2566).

187. Attend dancing and games at the annual Basque picnic sponsored by the Southern California Eskualdun Club (714/983-7553) on the first weekend of July at the Chino Fairgrounds, Edison Street and Central Avenue (714/861-0586).

188. In early July, dine on lamb and *cevapcici*, and dance to a *tamburitza* orchestra at the annual Croatian Festival held in Alpine Village Park, 833 W. Torrance Boulevard, Torrance (310/323-2872).

189. The ancient Japanese festival of *Tanabata*, the festival of the weaver, with *taiko* drummers and storytelling sessions, is held each July at the Pacific Asia Museum (46 N. Los Robles Avenue, Pasadena; 818/449-2742).

190. During the summer, attend the Day of the Lotus Festival at Echo Park Lake, Glendale Boulevard at Bellevue Avenue, highlighted by floral and art displays, dragon boat races, martial arts, music and dances of Asia and Polynesia (213/485-4825).

191. In August celebrate the Cambodian festival of *Chol Vassa* at the Khemara Buddhikorama, a social center for the preservation of Cambodian culture (2100 W. Willow Street, Long Beach; 310/595-8555).

192. Visit the Koyasan Buddhist Temple at 342 E. 1st Street (213/624-1267) and tour Little Tokyo during Nisei Week in August: *ondo* dancing, *bonsai* exhibits, and the opening of *sake taru*, a barrel of rice wine (Japan-American Cultural Center, 244 S. San Pedro Street, Los Angeles; 213/687-7193).

193. In mid-August celebrate *Chusak*, Korean Thanksgiving Day, by witnessing the annual parade and visiting the Korean Cultural Center (3350 Wilshire Boulevard, Los Angeles; 213/384-1924), and touring Koreatown, bounded by Hoover and 8th Streets and Olympic and Crenshaw Boulevards. Dine at Woo Lee Oak of Seoul, 623 S. Western Avenue (213/384-2244).

194. In late August mark Samoan Flag Day by attending the annual festival in Carson with coconut and banana peeling contests and cricket matches. Learn about L.A.'s Samoan community, the largest in the world outside Samoa itself (Samoan Affairs, Central Region: 310/538-0555).

195. Join the Chino Basque Club on Labor Day weekend for their annual picnic at the Chino Fairgrounds, Edison Street and Central Avenue (714/861-0586).

196. In September attend the traditional Scandinavian marketplace at Vass Park (2854 Triunfo Canyon Road, Agoura: 310/670-6018), with lace-making and glass sculpture demonstrations. Get there in time for the hearty Swedish breakfast.

197. In September participate in a Polish Harvest Festival with folk music and dancing, displays and dinner at Our Lady of Bright Mount (*Jasna Gora*) Church, 3424 W. Adams Boulevard (213/734-5249).

A Polish Festival is also held at the John Paul II Polish Center, 3999 Rose Drive, Yorba Linda in Orange County (714/996-8161).

198. Mark Columbus Day on October 12 with a tour of historic Italian structures in El Pueblo Historic Park (213/680-2525), including the Pelanconi House and the Italian Hall. Conclude with a presentation on the Italians of Los Angeles at a luncheon at Little Joe's restaurant, 900 N. Broadway in the heart of the old Italian business district (213/489-4900).

199. Attend the Greek Festival of music, dance and crafts presented by St. Catherine's Church in Torrance (213/540-2434) on the first weekend of October, followed by a festive dinner at San Pedro's Papadakis Taverna (301 W. Sixth Street; 213/548-1186), famed for its dancing waiters.

200. Enjoy the barbecue, the *ceilidl* and the games of the annual Scottish Highland Games in early October at the Chino Fairgrounds (714/861-0586).

Also see section on Native Americans.

Notes

For Children and Grandchildren

We wandered about day after day, in the cool summer sunshine, -- so near the ocean that oppressive heat was rare. As soon as breakfast was over, away we went. I was clad in a daily clean blue-and-white checked gingham apron, Harry, although but seven, in long trousers, "like the men." We romped in barn and garden, visited the corrals or gathered the eggs; we played in the old stage left in the weeds outside the fence, or worked with the tools in the blacksmith shop. When the long tin horn sounded at noon the call for the men's dinner, we returned to the house to be scrubbed. I was put into a white apron for mealtime, but back into my regimentals as soon as it was over. A second whitening occurred for supper and lasted until bedtime.

Sarah Bixby Smith, *Adobe Days* (1987).

201. Take an "Only in L.A." tour: Begin with a visit to the Farmer John murals in Vernon along the 3000 block of E. Vernon Avenue and on adjoining Soto and Downey Streets, followed by a drive by the Coca Cola Bottling Co. at 1334 S. Central Avenue (not presently open to tours) with its nautical details. After box lunches and cokes, proceed to the Bob Baker Marionette Theatre, 1345 W. 1st Street at Glendale Boulevard (213/250-9995).

202. Explore a Fairy Tale World: Drive by the "Witch's House," a Hansel and Gretel structure once part of a Hollywood movie set and since 1926 a private home, at 516 Walden Drive & Carmelita Avenue in Beverly Hills; known as the Spadena House, it was designed by Henry Oliver. Wander through Angel's Attic doll museum, 516 Colorado Avenue in Santa Monica (310/394-8331). Stop in Culver City at the Medieval-style apartments at 3819-25 Dunn Drive, one block from the center of town (secure permission first), and then proceed to an ice cream social at the MGM Studios, 10000 Washington Boulevard (310/280-6000).

203. Introducing Leo Politi: After attending the Holy Saturday blessing of the animals and viewing Politi's mural facing the Plaza in El Pueblo Historic Park

(213/680-2525), gather in the Placita de Dolores or in Father Serra Park for refreshments. Bring an exhibit of Politi's books, and read aloud from *Pedro of Olvera Street* and *The Story of Bunker Hill*.

204. Back to Mission Days: Tour San Fernando Mission, 15151 San Fernando Mission Boulevard in Mission Hills (818/361-0186), followed by refreshments and selected readings from *The Indians and the California Missions* by Linda Lyngheim, and *Sally and Father Serra* by Sarah Duque.

205. Christmas Then and Now: Plan a holiday visit to the gaily decorated Banning Mansion, 401 E. M Street in Wilmington (310/548-7777), for a round of old-fashioned games and a session in the antique school house, followed by a tour of the modern Mattel toy factory (333 Century Boulevard, El Segundo; 310/524-2000).

206. We're Off to See the Wizard: Visit the Rustic Canyon log cabins, originally part of the *Miles Standish* movie set, then proceed to the clubhouse, site of the original Uplifters Club whose organizers included L. Frank Baum, author of the Oz books (Rustic Canyon Recreation Center, 601 Latimer Road, Los Angeles; 310/454-9872). Enjoy readings from a selection of his writings, followed by refreshments, and possibly an Oz puppet show or a screening of *The Wizard of Oz*.

207. Toys! Toys! Toys!: Spend the afternoon at the Hobby City Doll & Toy Museum, 1238 S. Beach Boulevard, Anaheim (714/527-2323). Housed in a half-scale model of the White House, the museum contains more than 3000 dolls and toys.

208. Discover the Past: Visit the Discovery Museum of Orange County in the restored Victorian home of Hiram Clay Kellogg, where they may play with toys from bygone eras, be photographed in vintage clothes, explore an old-time classroom, use a washboard, churn butter, and play the antique square grand piano. The facility may also be reserved for Victorian birthday parties (3101 W. Harvard Street, Santa Ana; 714/540-0404).

209. Things That Go Bump in the Night: Young people 10 to 15 can celebrate Halloween by attending a special effects workshop where they will learn to make monsters and ghouls (Paramount Ranch 818/888-3770).

210. Open Their Eyes to the World: Visit a children's participatory museum with its exciting and imaginative possibilities. They may put on real firefighter's "turnouts," watch themselves as they perform on closed-circuit TV, act on a stage in Shakespearean costume, or experience centrifugal force in a spinning chair:

The Los Angeles Children's Museum, 310 N. Main Street (213/687-8800) has many interactive exhibits. The museum also offers tours, visiting twenty-four scheduled sites ranging from a violin-maker's shop to a bakery, an oil refinery to Dodger Stadium (213/687-8226).

Kidspace, 390 S. El Molino in Pasadena (818/449-9143) is a hands-on environment, entirely action-oriented, and staffed by helpful and encouraging docents.

The Children's Museum at La Habra, housed in a 1923 Union Pacific Railroad Station at 301 S. Euclid Street 3103/905-9793), includes a Preschool Playpark for infants and toddlers.

211. Talk to the Animals: In June take a Chino Dairy Tour (714/627-6177). Visit the W.K. Kellogg Arabian Horse Stables on the campus of Cal Poly, 3801 W. Temple, Pomona (714/869-2224); horse shows are held on weekends. Ask directions to Cal Poly's "Ag Valley" to visit other barnyard favorites.

212. People from History Books: Discover George Stuart's three-dimensional doll-sized portraits of more than 200 historical figures, each handmade in painstaking detail and dressed with historical accuracy. Call his Ojai gallery for reservations and directions (McNell and Reeves Roads; 805/646-6339). Some of the figures may also be seen at the Ventura County Museum of History and Art, 100 E. Main Street, Ventura (805/653-0323).

213. Children of Other Lands: Attend the Children's Sunday Summer Festival at the Junior Arts Center, Barnsdall Park. Activities range from Korean, Polynesian and Ugandan music and dance to the creation of East In dian spirit rattles, Japanese origami cranes and African dolls (213/485-4474).

214. Tell Them a Story: The following children's book stores have regularly scheduled storytelling:
Children's Book & Music Center, 2500 Santa Monica Boulevard, Santa Monica (310/829-0215),
Happily Ever After, 2640 Griffith Park Boulevard, Los Angeles (213/668-1996), and
Pages, 18399 Ventura Boulevard, Tarzana (818/342-6657).

215. Castles Fit for a Queen (or King): Browse through books on Victorian architecture, or take a walk through an historic architectural district. Then head for one of the many summer sand castle building contests. San Diego's Kids 'n Castles Competition for children under 12 is held at Imperial Beach in July (619/424-6663). For additional contests consult Outing #142.

Notes

Landscape and the Environment

There is one subject upon which your true Californian never wearies of dilating: -- the climate of his country. Be it in the ice-bound regions of the Sierras at mid-winter; be it in the mighty Mojave desert at mid-summer; be it amid the rumbling earthquakes of the south, or the fogs and sand storms of the north, your informant, after mentioning all other advantages of this favored land will gravely finish the catalogue by reminding you, "And it is the most glorious climate in the world!"

Thompson and West, *History of Los Angeles County, California* (1880).

216. Plan on an all-day hike to fault watch in the San Gabriels with the Wilderness Institute (818/887-7831; $40 per person).

217. Learn a bit about Southern California's earthquake history from a member of the Department of Seismology at California Institute of Technology, 1201 E. California Street, Pasadena (818/795-6811).

218. Take a "Fun with Fossils" walk through the Emery Borrow Pit Fossil Site in Ralph B. Clark Regional Park, 8800 Rosecrans Avenue in Buena Park (714/670-8052), in which a paleontologist will point out 15,000-year-old fossil deposits of ground sloths, camels and elephants.

Or visit the famous Rancho La Brea Tar Pits and the George C. Page Museum in Hancock Park, 5801 Wilshire Boulevard at Curson (213/936-2230), and see the remains of L.A.'s first inhabitants.

The Raymond M. Alf Museum on the campus of Webb School traces the history of life on earth through the fossil record; the Hall of Fossil Footprints features the most complete display of animal footprints in the U.S. (1175 Base Line Road, Claremont, CA 91711; 714/624-2798).

219. Capture the changing drama of the Santa Monica Mountains by visiting the sound, film and light exhibit "Life from Fire" at the Los Angeles County Mu seum of Natural History, 900 Exposition Boulevard in Exposition Park, Los Angeles (213/744-3414). Also visit the recreation of a California Condor habitat in the Ralph W. Schreiber Hall of Birds.

At the east end of Exposition Park, experience one of the dramatic environmental films at the IMAX Theatre operated by the California Museum of Science & Industry (213/744-2014).

220. In the spring see California native plants in their full bloom at Rancho Santa Ana Botanic Garden, 1500 N. College Avenue in Claremont (714/625-8767), or at the Theodore Payne Foundation, 10459 Tuxford Street, Sun Valley (818/768-1802). From March through May the Foundation operates a hotline providing information on spring wildflower displays throughout southern California (818/768-3533).

221. Celebrate a California spring and see native plants used in a water-saving garden at the annual Garden Open House at El Alisal, Charles Lummis' former home and Historical Society of Southern California headquarters, 200 E. Avenue 43, Los Angeles (213/222-0546).

See more than 100 varieties of native plants at the Earthside Nature Center of the Girls' Club of Pasadena (818/796-6120).

222. Visit three westside gardens: the six-acre Virginia Robinson Gardens in Beverly Hills (call ahead for reservations: 310/276-5367); the eight-acre Mildred E. Mathias Botanical Gardens at the north end of the UCLA campus (310/825-1260); and the Hannah Carter Japanese Garden in Bel Air, also administered by UCLA (reservations: 310/825-4574).

Have luncheon at the Hotel Bel Air set amidst an 11-acre garden accented by a stream and swans. Or picnic at the 410-acre Doheny Ranch (409 Hillcrest Drive, Beverly Hills), location of many TV and film episodes; request a ranger-led tour of the ranch house. Also visit the William O. Douglas Outdoor Classroom on a part of the Doheny ranch property (access from 2300 Franklin Canyon Drive or 1936 Lakedrive; 310/858-3834).

223. Visit Japanese gardens at the Huntington Library (1151 Oxford Road in San Marino; 818/405-2100),

Descanso Gardens (1418 Descanso Drive off Verdugo Boulevard south of Foothill in La Canada; 818/790-5571), the New Otani Hotel (120 S. Los Angeles Street; 213/629-1200) and the Japanese Cultural Center (244 S. San Pedro Street; 213/628-2725). Lunch at one of the restaurants in Japanese Village Plaza near 2nd and Central, and invite comments by a landscape specialist.

224. In the spring, visit Glendora's famous bougainvillea -- the largest in the United States, it stretches through Bennett Avenue backyards from Pasadena Avenue east to Cullen. Also see the 100-year-old Moreton Bay fig tree in Big Tree Centennial Park at the corner of Santa Fe and Colorado, and the 400/600-year-old oak in front of the 1883 Bender home at 742 N. Rainbow Drive. Lunch at the North Woods Inn, 540 N. Azusa Avenue, Covina (818/331-7444).

Notes

Literature

In examining the writings of Americans from the time they first reached Southern California, when it was held by the Spaniards, it soon becomes clear that a number of indigenous themes emerged. One of these, developing in three phases, was the contrast between the Spanish and the Yankee ways of doing things. . . Another subject resulted from the fact that the most numerous and important of the mission Indian groups lived in the south; the tale of their mistreatment and neglect merges rather strangely into the growing interest in the Southwestern pueblo and nomadic Indians, who were extolled with increasing enthusiasm by Southern California explorers and writers as the area grew more sophisticated. The theme of aridity and its conquest also plays a very prominent part in the literature of Southern California; the subject ranges from the fanciful attempts to create a new Mediterranean culture to the drama of reclaiming and holding the desert.

Franklin Walker, *A Literary History of Southern California* (1950).

225. After renovations are completed (scheduled for spring, 1992) arrange with the University of Southern California to tour the impressive library of Villa Aurora, former Santa Monica home of internationally acclaimed author Leon Feuchtwanger (Feuchtwanger Institute for Exile Studies, USC: 213/743-8438, 310/274-2176; secure additional approval from the Head of Special Collections, Doheny Library, USC: 213/740-7173).

226. Take a look at Los Angeles mystery writers with a mean streets walking tour starting at Sunset and Fairfax (Neighborhood Place Project, 8571-1/4 Rugby Drive, West Hollywood, CA 90069; 310/657-3733).

Follow in the footsteps of author Raymond Chandler with a screening of Chandler's *The Big Sleep* at KCET's Little Theatre (213/666-6500).

A possible dining stop is the Far East Cafe, the restaurant in Little Tokyo patronized by Chandler.

227. At El Molino Viejo, 1120 Old Mill Road in San Marino (California Historical Society: 818/449-5450) celebrate the literary lights of the nearby suburbs by staging a mini-film festival of selections from Zane Grey's *Riders of the Purple Sage*, Edgar Rice Burroughs' *Tarzan* and Frank Baum's *Wizard of Oz*. Round out the afternoon with a look at the (1905) house at 396 Mariposa, Altadena, home of the Zane Grey family from 1918 to 1970.

228. Arrange a meeting at Fowler Brothers Book Store, established in 1888 (717 W. 7th Street, Los Angeles; 213/627-7846), featuring reminiscences by local book dealers. Have an autograph party featuring books by local historians.

229. In the Old Venice City Hall browse through the Beyond Baroque Bookstore, and attend the varied evening programs which range from poetry readings to concerts to historic film festivals. On Saturday afternoons members of the audience read from their own poetry (310/822-3006). To find out about other poetry reading programs in the Los Angeles area call 818/992-POEM.

Stop next door at the former Venice City Jail, now the home of the Social and Public Art Resource Center (310/822-9560).

230. Take a guided tour of the William Andrews Clark Library, housed in a stately *Italian Rennaissance* building at 2520 Cimarron, Los Angeles (213/731-8529). Arrange to view some of the 17th and 18th century manuscripts in the collection.

231. Plan a group reading from some of Earl Stanley Gardner's books at one of the many local bookshops specializing in detective and mystery stories (Mysterious Bookshop, 8763 Beverly Boulevard, Los Angeles; 310/659-2959).

232. Take a docent-led tour of the rare book collection at the Huntington Library, with special emphasis on the works of writer Mary Austin. Arrange for a presentation on the author by one of the resident scholars specializing in Austin's writing (1151 Oxford Road in San Marino; 818/405-2100).

233. Arrange a tour of the restored Pasadena Public Library, with an added request to view the special collections having to do with Southern California writers. Inquire about the possibility of viewing a film version of one of the stories in the library's theater (285 E. Walnut Street; 818/405-4607).

234. At the Rustic Canyon Recreation Center, site of the Uplifter's Club (601 Latimer Road, Los Angeles; 310/454-5734), stage a Southern California author's party, with guests invited to come dressed as characters from books written by Frank Baum, Zane Grey, Edgar Rice Burroughs and Jessamyn West.

235. In Tujunga visit the McGroarty Cultural Art Center and tour the 1923 home of U.S. Congressman, historian and journalist John Steven McGroarty (7570 McGroarty Terrace; 818/352-5285).

Notes

Music and Drama

The Unitarian Church on Third and Hill streets was the first real home of music in Los Angeles. . . And it was here we had our first high-brow lectures. Lew Wallace lectured on Ben Hur. Blind Tom gave us wonderful music. Ovid Musin played the violin, Bill Nye and James Whitcomb Riley gave monologues. Then came Simpson's Auditorium built by the Methodists, with the first big organ of note in the city. Six years ago all big musical events took place here. Schumann-Heink was first introduced to Los Angeles in this hall, as were Calve, Sembrich, and Paderewski. These were big days -- wonderful times!

Genevieve Powell-Bond, "Our First Theatricals and Showmen," *Los Angeles Times*, March 28, 1914.

236. Visit the Multicultural Music & Art Foundation Northridge (P.O. Box 101, Northridge, CA 91328; 818/349-3431), the studio of music ethnologist Elizabeth Waldo, for a California Indian and mission music concert; an alternate site would be San Fernando Mission, 15151 San Fernando Mission Boulevard, Mission Hills (818/361-0186).

237. Arrange with the Southwest Museum to hear Charles F. Lummis' pioneering wax cylinder recordings of Mexican-American music at Lummis' own home, "El Alisal," 200 E. Avenue 43 (Historical Society of Southern California: 213/222-0546).

238. In the appropriate setting of the Ebell Club at Lucerne and Wilshire Boulevards (213/931-1277), explore the musical life of 19th century Los Angeles with music librarian/historian Jeannie Poole of CSU Northridge, (818/885-1200).

239. Attend a Saturday concert at the downtown Orpheum Theatre at 630 S. Broadway (213/239-0939), featuring the Wurlitzer Theatre Pipe Organ presented by the Los Angeles Theatre Organ Society (818/766-0466); contact the California Society of Theatre Historians (2755 Medlow Avenue, Los Angeles, CA 90065) for additional information.

240. In the Dunbar Hotel, invite a music historian to explore Southern California's influence on the recording of jazz and Big Band music. The Dunbar is now used for low-income and elderly housing; the basement, first floor and mezzanine areas are to become a museum. The hotel opened as the Somerville in 1928, and was the site of the first NAACP national convention on the west coast. Renamed the Dunbar in 1929, it soon became known as "a cross between the Waldorf Astoria and the Cotton Club" and, hosting such black entertainers as Duke Ellington, Count Basie, Louis Armstrong, Billie Holiday and Lionel Hampton, it became the hub of Central Avenue's jazz scene of the '30s and pre-World War II '40s (4225 S. Central Avenue at 41st Street, Los Angeles; 213/233-7168).

Follow with a summer Sunday afternoon jazz concert at the Times Mirror Central Court of the L.A. County Museum of Art (LACMA, 5905 Wilshire Boulevard; 213/857-6000).

241. Visit the Hollywood Bowl Museum at 2301 N. Highland Avenue (213/850-2059) and lunch in the picnic area. Follow with a guided tour of the Brand Music Library, Brand Park, 1601 W. Mountain Street, Glendale. Conclude with a guided tour of the Ambassador College campus, including the Ambassador Auditorium and gardens (300 W. Green Street, Pasadena; 818/304-6166).

242. Take a guided tour of the Music Center, 135 N. Grand, Los Angeles (213/972-7483) and relive "Luncheon at the Music Center" with founding program host, Thomas Cassidy, who was also M.C. of the "KFAC Evening Concert" for forty-three years (818/892-7817). Have luncheon on the Music Center patio, or at the California Pizza Kitchen in Crocker Center. Follow with a Wednesday noon summer concert at the California Plaza amphitheater across the street (213/687-2000).

243. View the exhibit of studio sketches and the actual costumes worn in Hollywood movies at the Fashion Institute of Design, 911 S. Grand Avenue, Los Angeles (213/624-1200). Then enter into the fantasy of the theater by touting the Center Theater Group Costume Shop, which covers a full city block at 3301 East 14th Street (213/267-1230).

244. Picnic and enjoy a summer afternoon outdoor performance of a Shakespearean play at the Will Greer Theatricum Botanicum, 1419 N. Topanga Canyon Boulevard, Los Angeles (310/455-3723).

Or celebrate the Bard in the southland at a weekend summer Shakespeare performance at Citicorp Plaza, 7th and Figueroa, Los Angeles (213/489-1121; admission by donation of canned food for the homeless).

In San Diego, attend the summer festival of Shakespeare's works at the Old Globe Theater in Balboa Park (619/239-2255).

245. Take a pre-concert tour of the Arnold Schoenberg Institute (213/743-5362) as guests of the USC School of Music, with invited comments from the staff about Schoenberg and his Southern California students. A campus visit could include a tour of the Fisher Gallery (213/743-2799) and an arranged visit to the Hancock Memorial Museum, containing furnishings of an 1890s mansion modeled after the Villa de Medici (Trousdale Way at Childs Way, USC campus; 213/740-0433).

246. In July enjoy old-time American music and dance at the Banjo & Fiddle Contest and Square Dance Festival at El Camino College (16007 Crenshaw Boulevard at Redondo Beach Boulevard, Gardena; 310/532-3670 x3592).

Notes

Native Americans

Before the Indians belonging to the greater part of this country were known to the Whites, they comprised as it were one great Family under distinct Chiefs. They spoke nearly the same language with the exception of a few words; and were more to be distinguished by a local intonation of the voice than anything else.

Being related by blood and marriage, war was never carried on between them. When war was consequently waged against neighboring tribes of no affinity, it was a common cause.

Hugo Reid, *The Indians of Los Angeles County* (1926).

247. Caravan to China Lake to view the rock drawings of the Caso Range, sponsored by the Maturango Museum, 100 E. Las Flores Avenue at China Lake Boulevard in Ridgecrest (P.O. Box 1776, Ridgecrest, CA 93555; 619/446-6900).

248. Visit the Chumash Painted Cave State Historic Park (Painted Cave Road off San Marcos Pass, Highway 154 north from Santa Barbara). Contact the California Parks & Recreation Department: 805/967-3475.

249. Explore evidence of Chumash ethno-astronomy at Charmlee County Park, Encinal Canyon Road off Pacific Coast Highway, Malibu (213/738-2961). Invite an anthropologist or ethnologist to discuss the subject.

250. Contact the Cahuilla Tribal Council (619/325-5673) in order to visit sites in the Malki, Andreas and Murray Canyons. Include a visit to the Malki Museum on the Morongo Indian Reservation, 11-795 Fields Road, Banning, CA 92220 (714/849-7289).

251. In late May attend the colorful Corpus Cristi Fiesta at the *assistencia* San Antonio de Pala (north of SR 76 on Pala Mission Road) in northern San Diego County. The return trip on Highway 15 could include stops at the Temecula Creek Inn (44501 Rainbow Road, Temecula, CA

92390: 714/676-5631) and historic Temecula. Stop at the Old Town Temecula Museum (28670 Front Street; 714/676-0021).

252. Visit the recreated Indian dwelling at the Los Angeles State & County Arboretum, 301 N. Baldwin, Arcadia (818/446-8251), and learn about California Indians and the plants they used in an illustrated talk by a member of the Arboretum staff. Hear Native American music demonstrated in some of the recordings by music ethnologist Elizabeth Waldo using authentic Indian instruments.

253. Visit the Southwest Museum, the oldest private museum in Los Angeles (1914), atop a hill in the Highland Park district of Los Angeles (take Avenue 43 exit from Pasadena Fwy. 110). The four main exhibit halls are highlighted by one of the largest basketry collections in the United States. The Museum houses the Braun Research Library of 50,000 volumes on Native American and California history and a Museum Store offering books and native crafts (234 Museum Drive, Los Angeles, CA 90065; 213/221-2164).

In addition, the Museum maintains the Casa de Adobe, modeled after the 1850s adobe of Rancho Guojome, at 4605 N. Figueroa Street at the foot of the hill; contact the Museum for information.

254. Visit the Mojave River Valley Museum, 270 E. Virginia Way, Barstow: 619/256-5452). Arrange to have a desert ecologist serve as guide to historic sites along the Mojave River trail.

255. Tour the Antelope Valley Indian Museum with its collections representing various Indian groups (15701 E. Avenue M, Lancaster: 805/942-0662). If visiting in the spring, stop at the Antelope Valley Poppy Reserve (for directions: 805/724-1180, 942-0662).

A possible side trip would be a visit to the ruins of Llano del Rio, the utopian colony founded by socialist Job Harriman early in the 20th century (just north of Hwy. 138, Pearblossom Highway, eight miles west of the Llano Post Office).

Old West

Human life at this period was about the cheapest thing in Los Angeles, and killings were frequent. Nigger Alley was as tough a neighborhood, in fact, as could be found anywhere, and a large proportion of the twenty or thirty murders a month was committed here. About as plentiful a thing, also, as there was in the pueblo was liquor. This was served generously in these resorts, not only with respect to quantity, but as well regarding variety.

Harris Newmark, *Sixty Years in Southern California, 1853-1913* (1970).

256. Visit the Wells Fargo Museum, 333 S. Grand Avenue in downtown Los Angeles (213/253-7166).

Proceed to the Los Angeles County Museum of Natural History at the west end of Exposition Park (213/744-3466) for a visit to the California History Hall. Lunch at Margarita Jones, 3760 S. Figueroa, just east of the Park (213/747-4400).

257. Attend an old-fashioned ranch barbecue in September at the Centinela Adobe, 7634 Midfield Avenue, Westchester; ribs and chicken with all the trimmings are followed by a mouthwatering array of homemade cakes. The adobe, the Land Office/museum, and the adjoining Heritage & Research Center will be staffed by costumed docents (Centinela Valley Historical Society: 310/649-6272).

For more than 35 years the La Puente Valley Historical Society has held a steak barbecue in early October (La Puente Valley Historical Society, P.O. Box 522, La Puente, CA 91747; 818/336-2382).

Another annual barbecue is held in October at the Louis Phillips Mansion, 2640 Pomona Boulevard, Pomona (Historical Society of Pomona Valley: 714/623-2198).

Or, have the famous "cactus stew" with tortillas and beans at the celebration of Rancho Days each September at the Andres Pico Adobe, 10940 Sepulveda Boulevard in Mission Hills (San Fernando Valley Historical Society: 818/365-7810). Demonstrations, crafts and a book sale are included in the festivities.

258. Join a hayride at the Old West Stables in Corona, which visits historical points of interest in Riverside County, including the site of the old Butterfield Stage Depot, followed by a chili dinner and country music (714/371-0161).

259. Prospect for gold at Fellows Camp on the east fork of San Gabriel Canyon, fifteen miles north of Azusa, where each spring the camp owner conducts a Treasure Hunters' Rendezvous. Dine at El Encanto, located on the site of old Camp One in San Gabriel Canyon, a restaurant since the 1930s (100 E. Old San Gabriel Road, Azusa: 818/969-8877).

260. Take a docent-led tour of the 52,000-square-foot Gene Autry Western Heritage Museum at 4700 Zoo Drive in Griffith Park, Los Angeles (213/667-2000), with its collection of over 12,000 items; follow with a showing of an early Hollywood "western" in the museum's theater.

261. Calico, once an 1880s silver boom town located in a quiet canyon in the Calico Mountains, is now a commercially restored 60-acre site which becomes particularly lively during the Calico Hullabaloo each spring (10 miles north of Barstow, Ghost Town Road off Interstate 15: 619/254-2122).

Stop in Barstow to visit the Mojave Valley Museum, containing discoveries from the Calico Early Man Site (270 E. Virginia Way; 619/256-5452).

262. Visit the El Monte Museum, 3150 N. Tyler (818/444-3813), to investigate that town's claim as the official end of the Santa Fe Trail. Stop at Santa Fe Trail Historic Park on Santa Anita Avenue next to the fire station (818/444-3813); while there visit El Monte's first jail, built in 1890, and the Osmond Ranch House. Trace the route to Adobe de Palomares, 491 E. Arrow Highway in Pomona, a one-time trading post (Pomona Historical Society: 714/623-2198), and proceed to the Sycamore Inn, 8318 Foothill in Rancho Cucamonga (714/982-1104) operating for more than 130 years as a coaching station and now a restaurant.

Stop at the Workman & Temple Family Homestead Museum, 15415 E. Don Julian Road, City of Industry

(818/968-8492), once occupied by descendants of pioneers who traveled the trail in 1841.

263. Explore the experience of growing up on a California rancho while touring Rancho Los Cerritos at 4600 Virginia Road (310/425-8965) and Rancho Los Alamitos at 6400 Bixby Hill (310/431-2258), both in Long Beach. Invite comments by the site staff. Read aloud from Sarah Bixby Smith's *Adobe Days*, describing her childhood there.

264. Invoke the spirit of the Old West with a visit to the twenty larger-than-life Wild West statues in the Cleveland Park area of the Pierce College campus, 6201 Winnetka Avenue in Woodland Hills (818/347-0551).

Follow with a picnic at the Paramount Ranch with its movie set frontier town on Cornell Road off Kanan Road, Agoura, in the Santa Monica Mountains National Recreation Area (National Park Service: 818/888-3770).

265. Contact the Nautical Heritage Society Museum in the Dana Point Lighthouse, 24532 Del Prado, Dana Point, CA 92629 (714/661-1001, or 1-800-432-2201) to make reservations for a sail aboard the 94-foot schooner *Californian*, an authentic replica of a 1849 revenue cutter and California's tall ship.

266. A Bakersfield tour should include a visit to the Kern County Museum, 3801 Chester Avenue (805/861-2132). The fourteen-acre museum contains fifty-six buildings, depicting life in the late 19th and early 20th centuries.

Dine at a Basque restaurant: Woolgrowers at 620 E. 19th Street (805/327-9584), or the Pyrenees Cafe at 601 Sumner Street.

267. Witness Civil War battle reenactment held at Fort Tejon State Historic Park, a restored 1854-1864 U.S. Army Dragoon post, north of L.A. in Lebec on Interstate 5. Battle reenactments, military demonstrations and Living History programs are held April through October; inquire for dates (805/248-6692). Take a picnic lunch.

268. The legacy of Don Juan Forster includes a visit to his first ranch, San Juan Capistrano, and to his later Rancho Margarita y Las Flores, which includes the

125,000 acre Camp Pendleton (619/725-5566) as well as the Rancho Santa Margarita master-planned community, the O'Neill Ranch and the 30,000-acre preserve on the ranch. While viewing the camp, the largest Marine base in the nation, arrange to visit the Forster home, now the Commandant's residence, and the Amphibian Vehicle Museum (619/725-4111).

In San Juan Capistrano, visit the O'Neill Museum (Pryor House), a restored century-old building that serves as the headquarters of the San Juan Capistrano Historical Society (31831 Los Rios Street: 714/493-8444).

269. In October, attend the Western Daze festivities as guests of the San Dimas Historical Society (P.O. Box 175, San Dimas, CA 91773-0175; 714/592-3818).

270. Visit the Drum Barracks Civil War Museum at 1052 Banning Boulevard in Wilmington (310/548-7509). This is the only remaining building of 1862-1873 Camp Drum, established as a 60-acre Civil War garrison and depot, where you will see artifacts and weapons of the era.

You may also drive by the site of Camp Latham, a Civil War camp located on Overland Avenue south of Ballona Creek, now the location of a senior citizens' center.

271. Attend the annual camel races at Industry Hills Equestrian Center off Temple Avenue in the City of Industry (818/965-0861), preceded by a talk about historic camel driver Greek George at his gravesite in Founders Memorial Park, Broadway & Citrus in Whittier, near Pio Pico's "El Ranchito" at 6003 S. Pioneer Boulevard (310/695-1212). Invite comments by a local historian.

272. Visit Kern County's Cowboy Memorial & Library, a hands-on museum dedicated to preserving the heritage of the cowboy and the mountain man, on Walker Basin Road, Caliente (Star Route, Box 68-A, Caliente, CA 93518: 805/867-2410).

Also in Kern County visit the Twenty Mule Team Museum, documenting a unique phase of frontier transportation (26962 Twenty Mule Team Road, Boron, CA 93516: 619/762-6253).

273. Take a two-hour covered wagon tour through the desert sands of the 13,000-acre Coachella Valley Preserve (Covered Wagon Tours, P.O. Box 1106, La Quinta, CA 92253: 619/347-2161).

274. Experience life on a western cattle ranch at the Quarter Circle U Rankin Ranch, established in 1863. Activities include horseback riding, hayrides and square dancing (Box 36, Caliente, CA 93518: 805/867-2511).

275. Attend Brawley's Cattle Call in November: western parade, bluegrass bands, dancing, chuckwagon breakfast, barbecues and an authentic PRCA Championship Rodeo -- all in the heart of a valley of ranches and agricultural communities (Information: 619/344-3160 -- Rodeo Tickets, P.O. Box 1336, Brawley, CA 92227; 619/344-5206)

276. Mark Memorial Day weekend with three-day Grubstake Days in Yucca Valley, an area rich in mining and ranching heritage. A parade, rodeo, race and traditional recreations highlight this 41-year-old celebration. Take Highway 62 north to Yucca Valley (619/365-6323).

277. Join the Joshua Tree Natural History Association guides for a 90-minute tour of the Desert Queen Ranch, also known as the Keys Ranch. The 160-acre facility, in operation from 1917 to 1969, was the most successful attempt at homesteading in the Morongo Basin.

Learn about gunfighters and goldminers during a two-hour ranger led tour of the Wall Street Mill located in the Hidden Valley area of Joshua Tree National Monument. Write: 74485 National Monument Drive, Twentynine Palms, CA 92277.

278. In Desert Hot Springs visit Cabot's Old Indian Pueblo, a four-story structure with 35 rooms and 150 windows built in Hopi Indian style by Cabot Xerxa. It now houses his personal museum (67-616 E. Desert View Avenue; 619/329-7610).

279. Relive the mining bonanza days in Randsburg and neighboring Johannesburg and Red Mountain. The faded buildings still reflect their 100-year history. A general store is still open at 35 Butte Avenue. The Desert

Museum in Randsburg traces the region's three waves of
prosperity generated by the discovery of gold, tungsten
and silver (619/374-2418).

Notes

Transportation

Whatever glass and steel monuments may be built downtown, the essence of Los Angeles, its true identifying characteristic, is mobility. Freedom of movement has long given life a special flavor there, liberated the individual to enjoy the sun and space that his environment so abundantly offered, put the manifold advantages of a great metropolitan area within his grasp.

Richard Austin Smith, *Fortune*, March 1965.

280. Early Los Angeles on the move: visit the 1904 Watts Train Station & Museum, 1686 E. 103rd Street at Grandee Avenue.

Tour the Railroad Museum at 250th Street & Woodward Avenue in Lomita (310/326-6255), and the nearby *Greek Revival* Banning Residence Museum at 401 E. M Street in Wilmington (310/548-7777), estate of transportation pioneer Phineas Banning. The Coach House with various types of wagons and coaches may be seen by arrangement.

281. Book a slide show about Mt. Lowe (Pasadena Historical Society: 818/577-1660). Picnic in Pasadena's Oak Grove Park, where the U.S. Forest Service/Angeles National Forest Ranger Station has an excellent brochure to supplement the material at each of ten interpretive stations along the Mt. Lowe Railroad Self-Guiding Trail; the brochure also contains a brief history of the Railway. Follow with a reading of the play *The Testing of Professor Lowe*.

282. Study the impact of the auto on drive-ins and drive-throughs, beginning with the refurbished Chapman Park Market, 3465 W. 6th Street, Los Angeles, a pioneer among auto malls. Continue on to nearby *Art Deco* I. Magnin Wilshire (formerly Bullock's Wilshire) at 3050 Wilshire Boulevard, the first department store to be oriented toward the parking lot (Magnin's tour by L.A. Conservancy: 213/623-CITY); lunch upstairs in the 1926 "Bullock's Tea Room" (Blum's: 213/387-4111).

283. Visit the 62-acre Orange Empire Railway Museum, 2201 South A Street, Perris (P.O. Box 548, Perris, CA 92370-0548; 714/657-2605), with more than 140 pieces of railroad stock and 35 Big Red Cars, all on display on six miles of track. Several historic streetcars and interurban trains operate on weekends, and train excursions are held during the April Rail Festival and the Fall Festival in October.

284. Visit the American Hall of Aviation History at Northrop University on Arbor Vitae near Aviation Boulevard in Inglewood, followed by lunch at the Proud Bird located above the LAX runway. Arrange with the Photo Collections Librarian at the Los Angeles Public Library (213/266-0779) for an illustrated lecture on pioneer aviation in Southern California.

Proceed to the 1827 Manuel Dominguez Adobe (Rancho San Pedro), 18127 S. Alameda Street in Compton (310/631-5981), site of Southern California's first international air race. One of the earliest Spanish land grants in California, the rancho was bequeathed by Dominguez to his daughters. The Adobe museum contains artifacts of the 1910 Dominguez Air Meet.

285. View the exhibits on the history of aviation and space at the Museum of Flying, 2772 Donald Douglas Loop North, Santa Monica (310/392-8822). Lunch at the adjacent DC-3 Restaurant.

286. Attend a monthly "Family Night" at Rockwell International, 12214 Lakewood Boulevard in Downey (310/922-3507). A film and speaker are featured, and you may view a mock-up of the Apollo XIV Command Module and a full scale space station.

287. Visit the Otis Chandler Auto Collection in Oxnard (Historic Motor Car Association, P.O. Box 30628, Santa Barbara, CA 93105; 805/966-9151).

Plan the visit to coincide with the vintage car races scheduled by the Association in late July.

288. Visit Vandenburg Air Force Base near Lompoc, especially in September or April, for a tour of the space shuttle facility. A day long visit should also allow time to visit some of the over 600 Chumash Indian sites on the base. Call thirty days in advance to make reservations: 805/866-1922.

289. Visit the Minter Field Air Museum at Shafter Airport in Bakersfield, a World War II Air Force training base with vintage aircraft, vehicles and artifacts (Rt. 11 -- Box 626, Bakersfield, CA 98312: 805/393-0291).

290. Investigate the various means of overland travel used by western pioneers at the Gilman Ranch Historic Park & Wagon Museum, at the corner of Wilson and 16th Streets in Banning (714/922-9200). Monthly walks and interpretive programs are also available.

291. Traveling in San Diego: visit Balboa Park for tours of the Aerospace Historical Center in the Ford Building (619/234-8291), which includes the Aerospace Museum and the national Aerospace Hall of Fame, and of the San Diego Automotive Museum (619/231-AUTO) with more than sixty cars on display -- from an 1886 Benz to a 1981 Delorean. Lunch at Casa del Prado in Balboa Park.

In May, vintage car races take place at the Jack Murphy Stadium in Mission Valley.

292. Take a 90-minute guided tour of the NASA Ames-Dryden Flight Research Facility on Edwards Air Force Base, Highway 14 in Lancaster, where NASA develops and tests new designs in aircraft (805/258-3446).

On return, stop at the restored Western Hotel in Lancaster, boardinghouse for early railroad construction workers (Western Hotel Historical Society, P.O. Box 304, Lancaster, CA 93534).

Women

Some of the artisans brought wives and families to keep them company. These women became active members of the frontier society. Wives and families augmented the family income through their work raising stock or harvesting crops. The women also bore children who increased the population. Thus the presence of women was equally vital to two of these settlement attempts. Women were settlers in their own right. Without women, the settlement activity would not have been successful. Their experience was as much a part of the military/settlement plan Galvez began implementing as was the men's experience. They were an integral part of the response to the petition for settlers which was echoed by administrators, military and missioners.

Salome Hernandez, "No Settlement Without Women: Three Spanish California Settlement Schemes, 1790-1800," *Southern California Quarterly*, Fall 1990.

293. Take a bus tour of historic sites associated with women of Los Angeles (tour guide from Cal Poly Pomona History Department: 714/829-3860).
Or invite a representative from the Power of Place Project, UCLA School of Urban Planning (310/825-8957),to lead a tour of Los Angeles sites significantly associated with the history of women.

294. At the 1912-13 Mary Andrews Clark Memorial Home YWCA (306 Loma Drive; 213/483-5780) plan a panel presentation honoring women city-builders of Los Angeles. Consult recent issues of scholarly journals for panelists who will speak on suffragist Caroline Severance, agriculturist Jeanne Carr, child welfare reformer Florence Edson, African-American newspaper publisher Charlotta Bass and various women philanthropists.

295. Invite a spokesperson from the UCLA Women's Studies Center (310/825-4601) to lead a tour of the Biddy Mason Memorial at 2nd and Spring Streets, followed by an illustrated lecture on this African-American slave who became a successful businesswoman and philanthropist. A possible venue would be the auditorium of the

Los Angeles Public Library, located not far from Biddy Mason's former land holdings (213/612-3314).

296. Trace women's lives through their quilts in the Margaret Cavigga Collection (8648 Melrose, Los Angeles; 310/659-3020), and a docent-led tour of the quilt collection at the Los Angeles County Museum of Art (LACMA, 5905 Wilshire Boulevard, Los Angeles; 213/857-6108).

297. On a visit to the Monterey Park Historical Society Museum (in Garvey Ranch Park, Orange Grove Avenue; 818/307-1267) arrange to view the video on local potato chip pioneer, Laura Scudder. Contact the public relations offices of Marie Callender's Restaurants (714/542-3355) and of Mrs. Sees Chocolates (310/559-4911) for materials and possible presentations on these two local businesswomen. Also contact Knott's Berry Farm (Buena Park; 714/220-5200) for information on Mrs. Knott, the creator of the boysenberry pie and the original cook at the Knott's farm restaurant.

298. Plan an outing to Caltech for a performance of the Coleman Music Concerts (818/356-3847), first organized by Alice Coleman Batchelder of Pasadena. Precede the concert with a presentation on the Los Angeles Women's Orchestra by Jeannie Poole, music librarian and researcher at Cal State Northridge (818/885-1200).

299. Arrange with Occidental College to tour the campus areas designed by landscape architect Beatrix Farrand (213/259-2751).

Invite authors of books and articles on the following to speak: agriculturists Jeanne Carr and Harriet Strong, horticulturist Kate Sessions, and landscape architects Lucille Council and Florence Yoch.

300. Tour the Pasadena YWCA (78 N. Marengo Avenue; 818/793-5171), one of several YWCAs including facilities in Hollywood and San Pedro designed by Julia Morgan, who was also the architect for the Los Angeles Examiner building and the Hearst estate, San Simeon. Follow with a slide presentation on the history of Los Angeles women with local women's historian Gloria Ricci Lothrop (714/629-2301).

301. Explore the past through the watercolors of Eva Scott Fenyes at the Southwest Museum (213/221-2163) high above the Pasadena Freeway 110 in Highland Park; then take a guided tour of her former home, now the headquarters of the Pasadena Historical Society, 170 N. Orange Grove Boulevard (818/577-1660).

302. With the assistance of the Music Department of Pasadena City College take a multi-media excursion through the history of Southern California modern dance (Dennies T. Barber: 818/578-7208).

303. Attend a slide show and display highlighting the contributions of Helen Petrovna Blavatsky, founder of the Theosophical Society, at its international headquarters (643 Mariposa, Altadena; 818/797-7817).

This could be combined with a presentation on the dynamic media evangelist Aimee Semple McPherson. Consult recent journal articles for a speaker. Tours of Angelus Temple, her church headquarters, may be arranged (1100 Glendale Boulevard, Los Angeles, CA 90026; 213/484-1100).

304. Visit Scripps College in Claremont, endowed by newspaperwoman and philanthropist Ellen Browning Scripps in 1926 for the education of young women. Note the inscriptions and *bas reliefs*, as well as the generations of messages inscribed on Senior Wall by graduates. Arrange to view Ellen Browning Scripps memorabilia and archival material in Dennison Library, as well as the extensive collection on history of women in the west (Columbia Avenue at Tenth Street, Claremont; 714/621-8000). Visit the nearby Sugg House designed by architect Helen Wren in her characteristic *Anglo-Colonial* style (NW corner 7th Street and Harvard Avenue). Stop at the Vivian Webb Chapel, a tiny mission-style church constructed of handmade adobe bricks, atop the Webb School campus (1175 W. Baseline Road, Claremont).

305. Explore the place of women in Southern California labor history with a representative of the Power of Place Committee, Urban Planning Department, UCLA (310/825-8957).

III. HOLIDAYS & DATES

A Calendar of Celebrations

> *A proclamation,* H. Ex. Doc. 31, i, no. 17, p. 867, *was issued by Governor C. Bennett Riley, setting apart the 29th day of November, 1850, to be kept in making a general and public acknowledgement of gratitude to the Supreme Ruler of the universe for his kind and fostering care during the year that was past.*
>
> Hubert Howe Bancroft, *History of California*, I: 306, n. 93 (1884).

306. Start the New Year right by attending the Tournament of Roses Parade in Pasadena, a Southern California tradition for over 100 years (Sharp Seating Company, 709 E. Colorado Boulevard, Pasadena, CA 91102-0068; 818/795-4171 -- or make arrangements with one of the many travel agencies which organize bus trips to the parade site). For two days following the parade, floats may be seen along Sierra Madre Boulevard between Paloma Street and Sierra Madre Villa Avenue, and along Washington Boulevard.

307. Celebrate the birthday of Robert Burns on January 25 with a poetry reading at Wee Kirk O' the Heather at Forest Lawn, Glendale (213/254-3131) and "the taking of the haggis" at the nearby Tam O' Shanter Inn, 2980 Los Feliz Boulevard (213/664-0228).

308. Celebrate Lincoln's birthday in Redlands with a tour of the Lincoln Memorial Shrine of the A.K. Smiley Library (125 W. Vine Street; 714/798-7565). Dine at Joe Greensleeves, 222 N. Orange (714/792-6969), housed in an 1890s building.

309. Check on the Presidents' Day activities scheduled at the Hall of Liberty and the Washington Monument at Forest Lawn Hollywood Hills (6300 Forest Lawn Drive, Los Angeles; 213/254-7251, 818/984-1711). It is possible to view the magnificent mosaic of "The Birth of Liberty," which tells the story of our nation's history from 1619 to 1787, and see Revolutionary War memorabilia in the Hall of Liberty

Note: Facilities at all five Forest Lawn Memorial Parks are available to organizations without charge for non-profit purposes.

310. Make Valentine's Day more memorable by perusing the valentine collection at the Grier-Musser Museum/mansion at 403 S. Bonnie Brae Place, Los Angeles (213/413-1814). English high tea and harp music round out the afternoon.

March is Women's History Month. See special section on Women's History.

311. In honor of April Fools Day, arrange a visit to the Banana Museum on N. El Molino Avenue in Altadena, containing over 15,000 banana artifacts (818/798-2272). Follow with -- what else? -- old fashioned banana splits at the Rose City Diner, a '50s era theme eatery (45 S. Fair Oaks Avenue in Old Town Pasadena; 818/793-8282).

312. Celebrate Mardi Gras with a tour of Center Theater Group Costume Shop, which covers a full city block at 3301 East 14th Street, Los Angeles (213/267-1230).

313. Usher in Easter with the famed Trombone Choir at the Moravian Church at 10337 Old River School Road in Downey (310/927-0718).

314. Attend the Easter Sunday Victorian apparel parade on Carroll Avenue, Los Angeles, followed by high tea at the nearby Sheraton Grande Hotel, 333 S. Figueroa (213/617-1133).

315. Celebrate John Muir's birthday on April 23 by attending the Wilderness Fair and Barbecue at Calamigos Ranch in the Santa Monica Mountains (818/887-7831). Contact the Sierra Club about a presentation on John Muir (3530 W. 6th Street, Los Angeles; 213/387-4287).

316. Honor *Cinco de Mayo* -- celebrating the victory of the Mexican forces under General Ignacio Saragosa against the French occupation of Mexico, in battle of Puebla on May 5, 1862 -- with a visit to the Museum of Mexican Heritage at Forest Lawn Hollywood Hills, 6300 Forest Lawn Drive (213/254-7251, 818/984-1711).

Follow with a stop at Olvera Street, El Pueblo de Los Angeles, where this celebration is always colorful (213/680-2525).

317. Mark Mother's Day with the Monrovia Home Tour sponsored by the Monrovia Old House Preservation Group, (P.O. Box 734, Monrovia, CA 91017; 818/358-7822). There will be musical entertainment and craft booths, and a luncheon is also available.

Round out the afternoon by attending the vintage fashion show at Heritage Square Museum at 3800 Homer Street (Avenue 43 exit from Pasadena Fwy. 110; 818/358-3129).

318. Attend the annual celebration of Israel's Independence Day in May/June at Rancho Park, Pico Boulevard and Motor Avenue, Los Angeles (Jewish Commmunity Centers Association: 213/938-2531).

319. Celebrate the Summer Solstice (occurs June 21 or 22) at the Folk Music and Dance Festival sponsored annually by the California Traditional Music Society (818/342-SONG).

320. During Maritime Week in early June tour naval warships stationed at Los Angeles Harbor, San Pedro, followed by harbor excursions and a visit to the Fort MacArthur Military Museum at 3601 S. Gaffey Street in Angels Gate Park (310/519-1875) for a presentation on military installations during World War II.

321. Attend the annual air show at El Toro Marine Air Station in June, featuring the famed "Blue Angels" precision flight team (714/651-3512).

322. Celebrate the Fourth of July by attending the annual Independence Day party, complete with square dancing and an antique engine show, at Stowe House, headquarters of the Goleta Valley Historical Society (304 N. Los Carneros Road, Goleta, CA 93117; 805/964-4407). While there, visit the Southern Pacific Depot, the Sexton

Agricultural Museum and the Goleta Valley Maritime Museum.

323. Experience the true spirit of '76 with a July 4th visit to Independence Hall at 8039 Beach Boulevard (across from Knott's Berry Farm entrance) in Buena Park. The exterior and interior are replicas of Independence Hall in Philadelphia. Inside the Declaration Chamber visitors may listen to a reenactment of the debates that proceeded the actual signing of the Declaration of Independence. In the lobby is a replica of the Liberty Bell (714/220-5200).

324. Celebrate Bastille Day on July 14 at Pioneer Boulangerie, 2012 Main Street in Santa Monica (310/399-7771). Arrange with a local university for a talk on the French in Southern California, or call El Pueblo Historic Park (213/680-2525).

325. March with the Pobladores-200 on Labor Day, as descendants of the founding families celebrate the September 4 birthday of the City of Los Angeles, following the trail of 1781 from Mission San Gabriel to El Pueblo Historic Park in Los Angeles (Los Pobladores, 10686 Meads Avenue, Orange, CA 92669).

326. The Festival of Masks is held at the Craft & Folk Art Museum, 5814 Wilshire Boulevard, Los Angeles (213/937-5544), and across the street in La Brea Tar Pits Park on the Sunday before Halloween. A parade is also scheduled.

327. To celebrate Halloween, take a guided twelve-block "ghost walk" of San Juan Capistrano, sponsored by the San Juan Capistrano Regional Library (714/834-6835).
Or, experience "Ghosts, Myths & Legends," exploring the world of strange phenomena, unexplained happenings and legendary celebrities aboard the *Queen Mary* in Long Beach (310/435-3511).

328. Take an October weekend trip to Ayers Pumpkin Patch to join in hayrides, harvest eight varieties of pumpkins and attend a Harvest Fair (Briggs and Telegraph Roads, Santa Paula; 805/525-9293).

329. To mark the arrival of water from the Owens Valley on Nov. 5, 1913 tour of the Castaic water plant near the Cascades site where William Mulholland first announced, "There it is, take it!" (Write: Castaic Lake Water Agency, 23560 W. Lyons Avenue, Newhall, CA 91321).

On the return trip take a guided tour of the Japanese Gardens at the Donald C. Tillman Water Reclamation Plant, 6100 Woodley Avenue, Van Nuys (818/989-8166).

330. Take a Veterans' Day tour of Camp Young off Interstate 10 at Chiriaco Summit, 28 miles east of Indio, where you can visit the headquarters of General George Patton's Desert Training Center. The museum contains a variety of World War II memorabilia, and also displays a massive topographical map prepared by the Metropolitan Water District, showing eleven former desert training camp sites and depicting the development of Southern California's water system (619/227-3227).

331. Make a Veterans' Day visit to the American Society of Military History & Museum, "Patriotic Hall," 1816 S. Figueroa, Los Angeles (213/746-1776), home of the first American Legion Post in the county.

Continue on to the Museum of World Wars and Military History, 7884 E. La Palma Avenue at Beach Boulevard, Buena Park (714/952-1776).

332. Recognize Veterans' Day with a visit to American Military Museum & Heritage Park, a seven-acre outdoor museum containing the largest military collection in the west (1918 N. Rosemead Boulevard, El Monte; 818/442-1776).

Follow with a guided tour of the Planes of Fame Air Museum with its collection of vintage aircraft (7000 Merrill by the Chino Airport; 714/597-3722). Many of the World War II planes take part in the annual Air Show in mid-May.

An alternative patriotic site would be the March Field Museum, which contains vintage aircraft, military uniforms and memorabilia. Planes in the flight line may be viewed by free bus tour (take Interstate 215, Moreno Valley, Riverside County; 714/655-3725).

333. Observe some of the Tournament of Roses parade floats in-the-making during the days immediately preceding the New Year's Day parade -- at Rose Palace, 835 S. Raymond Avenue, and/or Rosemont Pavilion, 700 Seco Street, both in Pasadena.

Follow with an afternoon at the Tournament Equestrian Festival, held at the L.A. Equestrian Center, 480 Riverside Drive at Main, Burbank (818/840-9066). For information on other Tournament activities, call: 818/449-ROSE.

Notes

Christmastime

Christmas was the greatest fiesta *of all and while there were not so many guests as on other occasions, because each rancho celebrated at home, nevertheless with the Indian retainers and travelers there was always a large gathering.*

It took weeks to prepare for Christmas. Presents must be made or unpacked, because when we wanted Christmas presents in Boston we had to send word eighteen months ahead by the captain of the hide boats that came to Monterey. . . Before Christmas the family amused themselves playing parlor games, story telling and dancing. The usual dainties to last until the new year were all prepared before hand so that it was easier to handle the Christmas and New Year's dinners while all the merrymaking was going on. Dancing . . . kept up, sometimes all night until after the New Year. The guitar and violin were usual musical instruments. The waltz was very popular, but during the early fifties the schottische *and* varsovienne *were introduced, much to the delight of the young people.*

Dr. Albert Shumate, editor, *Boyhood Days: Ygnacio Villegas' Reminiscences of California in the 1850s* (1983).

334. On Christmas Eve attend the Filipino *Panawagon* (a procession similar to Mexico's traditional *Las Posadas*), followed at midnight with *La Misa de Galo*, where communities compete to create the largest *parol* (lantern). For information contact: Philippine California Chamber of Commerce, 3350 Wilshire Boulevard, Los Angeles; 213/487-1937.

335. Celebrate Russian Orthodox Christmas with a demonstration of Ukrainian egg decorating (*pysanky*) and the making of bread, straw and ceramic decorations at the Ukrainian Art Center, 4315 Melrose Avenue, Los Angeles (213/668-0172). Following carols and a 17th-century Ukrainian puppet show, enjoy dinner and festive dancing at Ritza Russian Restaurant, 5468 Wilshire Boulevard (213/668-0172).

336. Learn about Southern California's Dutch population while celebrating a Netherlands Christmas at

Avio Clubhouse, 1557 W. Katella Avenue in Anaheim (310/ 941-5637). There will be *klompen* dancers, the Holland Choir and Dutch and Indonesian food.

337. Add a Bavarian German flavor to Christmas with a shopping expedition to Alpine Village at 833 W. Torrance Boulevard in Torrance (310/327-4384).

Follow with a gift bazaar and *smorgasbord* lunch at the Norwegian Seaman's Church, 1035 S. Beacon Street in San Pedro (310/832-6800).

338. Celebrate a Scandinavian Christmas with song and Nordic baked goods as guests of the Swedish-American Historical Association (c/o California Lutheran University, 60 W. Olsen Road, Thousand Oaks, CA 91360).

339. Walk through the Naples district of Long Beach -- particularly attractive at Christmas time! -- as guests of the Long Beach Historical Society (310/435-7511).

The Long Beach Christmas parade of boats (310/ 435-4093) may be viewed best from Shoreline Village Marina, or from the *Queen Mary*.

340. Celebrate Christmas with a holiday tour of the Banning Residence Museum at 401 E. M Street in Wilmington (310/548-7777), followed by viewing of the "L.A. Harbor Christmas Afloat" parade of illuminated boats in San Pedro (310/498-9273), or by a visit to see the Christmas *luminarias* at the historic Centinela Adobe, 7634 Midfield Avenue, Westchester (Centinela Valley Historical Society: 310/649-6272).

341. In early December celebrate "Holidays in the Garden" at the South Coast Botanic Garden, 26300 Crenshaw Boulevard on the Palos Verdes Peninsula (310/377-0466). Demonstrations of holiday flower arrangements are followed by English high tea and live musical entertainment.

342. Choose a harborside restaurant for dinner -- Reuben E. Lee, (714/675-5790); John Domini's, (714/650-5112); Tale of the Whale, (714/673-5245) -- and to view the illuminated yacht parade at Newport Beach (Newport Beach Chamber of Commerce for date, time: 714/644-8211).

For information regarding additional Christmas boat parades call the following: Ventura 805/648-2075; Oxnard 805/984-3366; Marina del Rey 310/821-7614; San Pedro 310/498-9275, 831-3950; Long Beach 310/435-4093; Huntington Beach 714/840-7542; Dana Point 714/496-5794, 496-6040; and San Diego 619/234-4111.

343. Attend the traditional *Las Posadas* celebration at the Andres Pico Adobe, 10940 Sepulveda, Mission Hills (818/365-7810), or at Olvera Street in El Pueblo de Los Angeles (213/680-2525).

Traditional Christmas festivities, including luminaria displays, may be enjoyed at Casa Adobe de San Rafael, 1330 Dorothy Drive, Glendale (818/249-4350); the Centinela Adobe, 7634 Midfield Avenue, Westchester (310/649-6272); and the Dominguez Rancho, 18127 S. Alameda Street, Dominguez Hills (310/631-5981).

344. Plan a holiday luncheon in the Fenyes Mansion of the Pasadena Historical Society, 470 Walnut Street, Pasadena (818/577-1660).

Lunches may also be scheduled at the Banning Residence Museum, 41 E. M Street in Wilmington (310/548-7777) and at the Lummis House, headquarters of the Historical Society of Southern California, 200 E. Avenue 43 in the Highland Park section of Los Angeles (213/222-0546).

345. Celebrate Christmas at the Adamson House, decorated annually by the Malibu Historical Society, at 23200 Pacific Coast Highway (310/456-8432). Follow with a visit to the Country Christmas Village located on the 80-acre Calamigos Ranch (take Kanan-Dume Road, from Pacific Coast Highway or from Ventura Freeway 134, to Mulholland Highway and follow signs: 818/889-9724).

346. During the first two weeks of December, join in the celebration of a Country Christmas at Descanso Gardens, where newspaper publisher Manchester Boddy's historic home and grounds are festively accented by florists, interior designers and landscape experts. Include lunch and a visit to wreath-making demonstrations and the Descanso Guide boutique (1418 Descanso Drive, La Canada-Flintridge: 818/790-5571).

347. Visit the festively decked Queen Anne Cottage at the Los Angeles County Arboretum, 301 N. Baldwin Avenue, Arcadia (818/821-3222). The cottage has been restored and stands in memory of Lucky Baldwin's third wife, Jennie Decker. Follow with high tea at the Huntington Library & Gardens, scheduling the visit to coincide with the annual Christmas readings presented in the Overseers Room (1151 Oxford Road, San Marino, 818/405-2282; Tea Room reservations, 818/584-9337).

After sundown, take time to drive up "Christmas Tree Lane," Santa Rosa Avenue in Altadena, where thousands of colored lights illuminate the aged deodars (the seeds were brought from India in 1885) from mid-December through New Year's Eve.

348. Celebrate Christmas in the Inland Empire with a nostalgic visit to the Victorian three-story Christmas House Bed & Breakfast, 9240 Archibald Avenue, Rancho Cucamonga (714/980-6450). Then take luminaria tours of the restored Casa de Rancho Cucamonga (Rains Home) at Vineyard Avenue & Hemlock Street in Rancho Cucamonga (714/989-4970), and of the 1837 Casa Primera de Rancho San Jose, 1569 N. Park Avenue at McKinley (Historical Society of Pomona Valley: 714/623-2198). Conclude with a fireside dinner by candlelight at La Cheminee, 1133 W. 6th Street near Mountain in Ontario (714/983-7900).

349. Another Inland Empire tour could begin by experiencing a 1920s Christmas with a visit to the Workman & Temple Family Homestead Museum, 15415 E. Don Julian Road, City of Industry (818/968-8492). Stop at the El Monte Museum at 3150 Tyler Street to view exhibits of holiday table settings (818/444-3813). Visit Boys Republic where the famous Della Robbia Christmas wreaths are assembled (3493 Grand Avenue, Chino: 714/5591-9122).

Travel to Redlands to participate in the popular Christmas tour of decorated Victorian homes sponsored by the YWCA (16 E. Olive Avenue: 714/793-2957).

350. An Orange County Christmas could include a tour of the festively decorated Heritage House at the Fullerton Arboretum on the campus of Cal State Fullerton (714/773-3579). Visit with the costumed docents who interpret the history of the 1898 Newland House, the oldest home in Huntington Beach, at 19820 Beach Boulevard (714/962-4112).

Follow with a unique shopping spree through the forty specialty shops of Old World Village, 7561 Center Avenue, Huntington Beach (714/898-3033, 890-7100). If time permits, travel on to Heritage Hill Historic Park in El Toro (25151 Serrano Road: 714/855-2028), which reflects a traditional Christmas atmosphere.

351. Enjoy the beauty of Christmas at Rogers Gardens, 2301 San Joaquin Hill Road (714/640-5802) and the Sherman Library & Gardens, 2647 E. Coast Highway in Corona Del Mar (714/673-2261), where lunch may be served and the staff may be invited to comment on the historic collection.

Take an historical homes tour of Laguna Beach (714/497-3311), or Laguna's "Christmas by the Sea" home tour presented annually in early December (714/494-8533). If energy and time permit, watch the sunset from the Ritz Carlton, with its 50-foot Christmas tree, 9-foot-high gingerbread house and 100,000 twinkling lights (33533 Ritz Carlton Drive, Laguna Niguel: 714/240-2000).

352. In early December attend the Christmas Faire at Heritage Park Village, Peyri Road near Mission San Luis Rey, Oceanside (619/439-4323, 439-7290).

Participate in San Diego's Christmas on the Prado in Balboa Park, featuring a Santa Lucia candlelight procession, entertainment, crafts and ethnic foods (619/239-2001). Continue the holiday celebration at Old Town San Diego State Historic Park, with visits to La Casa de Machado & Stewart, La Casa de Estudillo and the elegant Casa de Bandini Cosmopolitan Hotel (619/237-6770).

353. Visit the festively decorated Stowe House, headquarters of the Goleta Valley Historical Society (304 N. Los Carneros Road, Goleta; 805/964-4407). In Santa Barbara attend a performance of *Una Pastorella*, a traditional shepherd's play presented in mid-December (805/962-8606).

354. Take the Christmas home tour sponsored by the Ojai Historical Society. Consult the Visitors Guide, Ojai Valley News, P.O. Box 277, Ojai, CA 93023 (1016 W. Ojai Avenue; 805/646-1476).

355. Celebrate Christmas in January by attending a Christmas celebration at an Orthodox church, such as the Ukranian Church of the Nativity of the Blessed Virgin Mary at 5154 De Longpre Avenue, Los Angeles (213/663-6307).

Notes

APPENDIX A. GUIDES

Self-Guided Tours: articles, brochures, maps

Beach
Towns

Robert Pierson, *The Beach Towns: A Walker's Guide to L.A.'s Beach Communities* (Chronicle Books).

Brea

Brea Walking Tour
Brea Civic Cultural Center
#1 Civic Center Circle
Brea, CA 92621

Claremont

Claremont Colleges Walking Tour
Claremont Historic Resources Center
590 W. Bonita
Claremont, CA 91711

Paul Faulstick, *A Guide to Claremont Architecture* (Claremont, 1977).

Downey

A Bicentennial Guide to Historic Sites
Downey Historical Society
P.O. Box 554 (12540 Rives Avenue)
Downey, CA 90241-0554
310/862-2777

Fullerton

Downtown Fullerton Walking Tour
City Hall, 303 W. Commonwealth
Fullerton, CA 92632
714/992-6882

Glendora

Historical Sites in Glendora
Glendora Historical Society
P.O. Box 532, Glendora, CA 91740

Hollywood

A Tribute to the Stars: Map to the Stars' Graves, Final Curtain, P.O. Box 8542
Mission City, CA 91346

Robert Pierson, "A Stroll Through Hollywood's Gaudy Era," *Los Angeles Times* (October 25, 1985) V-1.

_____, "Avenues of Design in West Hollywood," *Los Angeles Times* (March 25, 1989) V-14.

_____, "Historic District Tour," *Los Angeles Times* (October 25, 1986) V-1.

_____, "Hollywood History," *Los Angeles Times* (June 27, 1987) V-1.

_____, "Mean Streets Walking Tour," *Los Angeles Magazine* (January 1986) pp. 84-90.

Would You Believe Hollywood Boulevard?
The Los Angeles Conservancy, and
  The Hollywood Revitalization Committee
727 W. 7th Street #955
Los Angeles, CA 90017
  213/623-CITY

Laguna

Laguna Beach North: Self-Guided Tour
  and
Laguna Beach South: Self-Guided Tour
  City Hall, 505 Forest Avenue
  Laguna Beach, CA 92651

Lompoc

"Riding through time . . . and flower fields, the Lompoc Valley's long, flat country roads make for easy riding," *Sunset Magazine* (June 1991) pp. 16-17.

Long Beach

Robert Pierson, "Walking Tour of Naples Island Area," *Los Angeles Times* (December 20, 1986) V-1.

Los Angeles

Angelino Heights House and Walking Tour,
  Carrol Avenue Restoration Foundation
  1316 Carroll Avenue
  Los Angeles, CA 90026

Alvarado Terrace House Tour,
Buildings Reborn in Los Angeles,
Cruisin' L.A.
  and,

Would You Believe Los Angeles?
Los Angeles Conservancy
727 W. 7th Street #955
Los Angeles, CA 90017
213/623-CITY

Los Angeles Chinatown Walking Tour:
Yesterday and Today
CHSSC Publications c/o E. Quan
4205 S. La Salle Avenue
Los Angeles, CA 90062

Heritage Square (tour brochure)
Cultural Heritage Foundation
100 S. Los Robles #470
Pasadena, CA 91101-2453

Highland Park (tour brochure)
Highland Park Heritage Trust
P.O. Box 42894
Los Angeles, CA 90050-0894

"L.A. Museum Strategy Map," *Sunset*
Magazine (February 1991) pp. 22-23.

"Old books, rare books, musty or mint . . .
in L.A., Santa Barbara," *Sunset Magazine*
(February 1980) pp. 76-78.

Welcome to West Adams
West Adams Heritage Association
4311 Victoria Park Drive
Los Angeles, CA 90019
213/935-6335, 737-7817

Dolores Hayden, *Power of Place: Self-Guided*
Tour of Los Angeles Women's History
College of Environmental Design, UCLA

Elizabeth McMillian, *1929-1979 a*
Legend Still: Bullock's Wilshire
(Los Angeles, 1979).

Marilyn Oliver, "10 Movie Theatres That Exemplify an Opulent Architectural Tradition," *Los Angeles Times* (January 24, 1991) E-6.

Robert Pierson, "Century City," *Los Angeles Times* (January 30, 1988) V-1.

_____, "Boyle Heights," *Los Angeles Times* (May 2, 1987) V-1.

Malibu   _____, "4-Hour Tour of Malibu: Its Natural and Architectural Sites," *Los Angeles Times* (September 3, 1988) V-13.

Monrovia   *Old Monrovia House Tour*
Los Angeles Conservancy
727 W. 7th Street #955
Los Angeles, CA 90017
213/623-CITY

Newport/   Robert Pierson, "Beaches of Newport Bay,"
Balboa   *Los Angeles Times* (August 22, 1987) V-1.

_____, "The Trail for a Walk at Balboa Beach," *Los Angeles Times* (September 16, 1989) V-16.

Ojai   *Walking Tour of Ojai -- Map*
Ojai Realty Co.
260 E. Ojai Avenue
Ojai, CA 93023
805/646-4331

Orange   *City of Orange Walking Tour*
Orange Chamber of Commerce
80 Plaza Square
City of Orange, CA 92666
714/538-3581

Orange   *Orange County Centennial Historical Map*
County   Orange County Historical Commission
P.O. Box 4048
Santa Ana, CA 92702-4048

Robert Pierson, "History and Architecture of Orange County," *Los Angeles Times* (July 9, 1988) V-1.

Pacific
Palisades

_____, "Los Angeles Artists in Rustic Canyon," *Los Angeles Times* (November 21, 1987) V-1.

Palos
Verdes

_____, "Palos Verdes Estates," *Los Angeles Times* (March 21, 1987) V-1.

Pasadena

Neighborhood Walking Tours of:
  Ashtabula;   *Monk Hill*;
  Morengo;   *Orange Heights*;
  Villa Park;
Ten Tours of Pasadena;
    and
Walking Tour of Old Pasadena Alleyways
  City of Pasadena Urban Conservation
  City Hall, Room 111
  100 N. Garfield
  Pasadena, CA 91101
    818/405-4228

Pasadena: Self-Guided Auto Tours -- Map
  Pasadena Beautiful Foundation
  map available from Gamble House
  bookstore, 4 Westmorland Place
  Pasadena, CA 92103-3593

Robert Pierson, "Pasadena's Old Town," *Los Angeles Times* (February 20, 1988) V-1.

Self-Guided Tour of the Gamble House Area
  Gamble House Docent Council
  4 Westmorland Place
  Pasadena, CA 92103-3593
    213/681-6427, 818/793-3334

Some Victorians to See in Pasadena
  Cultural Heritage Program
  Dept. of Housing & Development
  100 N. Garfield Avenue
  Pasadena, CA 92101
    818/577-4206

Redlands	*A Walking Tour of Historic Downtown Redlands* City Clerk's Office, City of Redlands 30 Cajon Street, P.O. Box 3005 Redlands, CA 92373 714/798-7549
Redondo	"For strolling, fishing, dining, Redondo's old pier is still thriving," *Sunset Magazine* (August 1991) p. 23
San Diego	*Walks in San Diego County* series in San Diego Home/Gardens beginning May 1986
San Fernando Valley	*Guide to San Fernando Valley Landmarks* (a driving tour) San Fernando Valley Historical Society 10940 Sepulveda Boulevard Mission Hills, CA 91345 818/365-7810
Santa Barbara	*Red Tile Walking Tour* Visitor Center, 1 Santa Barbara Street Santa Barbara, CA 93101 805/965-3021 *Tour Map of Wineries and Vineyards* Santa Barbara County Vintners Association P.O. Box 1558 Santa Ynez, CA 93460 805/688-0881 *Walking Tours Through History* Santa Barbara Trust for Historic Preservation 915 Santa Barbara Street Santa Barbara, CA 93101
Santa Clarita Valley	*(tour brochure)* Santa Clarita Valley Historical Society P.O. Box 875 Newhall, CA 91322

Santa Monica	*Guide to Public Art in Santa Monica* Santa Monica Visitors Center 1400 Ocean Avenue Santa Monica, CA 90402
South Pasadena	"South Main Street, U.S.A., just 6 miles from L.A. City Hall," *Sunset Magazine* (June 1991) pp. 23-24.
Tustin	*Take Main Street to Tustin History* Tustin Museum Tustin Chamber of Commerce 395 El Camino Real Tustin, CA 92680 714/731-5701
Venice	Robert Pierson "History and Current Attractions of the Venice Area," *Los Angeles Times* (August 6, 1988) V-13.
Whittier	*Whittier Village Walking Tour* Whittier Historical Society & Museum 6755 Newlin Avenue Whittier, CA 90601 310/945-3871

General Guidebooks

American Library Association, Local Information Committee, *L.A. the Ethnic Place* (Los Angeles, 1983).

Appleburg, Marilyn, editor, *I Love Los Angeles Guide, The Ultimate Source Book for Natives & Visitors* (New York, 1987).

Atkinson, Janet L., *Los Angeles County Historical Directory* (Jefferson, NC, 1988).

Automobile Club of Southern California, *200 Treasures of Metropolitan Los Angeles* (Los Angeles, 1980).

Bakalinsky, Adah and Larry Gordon, *Stairway Walks n Los Angeles* (Berkeley,1990).

Barsky, Felicia and Wendy Patterson, "Building the State: Women's Historical Sites by County," *Social Studies Review: Journal of the California Council for the Social Studies* 29 (Fall 1989), pp. 14-23.

Bates, Colleen, editor, *The Best of Los Angeles*, revised ed. (New York, 1988).

Bemet, Morris and Sue, *Here's San Diego* (New York, 1980).

Bendes, Barry M., *San Diegan* (San Diego, 1990-91).

California Department of Parks and Recreation, *A Visitor's Guide to California State Parks* (Sacramento, 1990).

Camaro Editors, *Official Visitors Guide: Los Angeles* (Los Angeles, 1982).

Chapman, Marvey, *A Marmac Guide to Los Angeles*, Marmac Guide Series (Gretna, LA, 1988).

Chase, John, "Map Guide to Recent Architecture in Los Angeles," *L.A. Architect* 7 (October 1981), pp. 2, 7.

Clark, David L., *L.A. on Foot* (Los Angeles and San Francisco, 1972).

Daniel Freeman Hospital, *Accessible L.A.: A Guide to Los Angeles for the Physically Challenged* (Inglewood, 1987).

Department of Parks and Recreation, *California Historical Landmarks* (Sacramento, 1991).

Federal Writers' Project Staff, *Los Angeles: A Guide to the City & Its Environs*, American Guides Series (1941).

Foster, Lynne, *Adventuring in the California Desert* (San Francisco, 1987).

Gagnon, Dennis R., *Hike Los Angeles, Vol. 1* (1986).

_____ *Hike Los Angeles, Vol. 2* (1986).

Gebhard, David, "Los Angeles: An Architectural Tour," *Portfolios* 2 (September/October 1980), pp. 106-109.

Gebhard, David and Robert Winter, *Architecture in Los Angeles: A Compleat Guide* (Salt Lake City, 1985).

Gousha, H.M., *Spade & Archer's 50 Maps of L.A.* (New York, 1991).

Greater Los Angeles Visitors and Convention Bureau, *Los Angeles and Southern California Guide* (Los Angeles, 1990).

Grenier, Judson A., Doyce B. Nunis, Jr., and Jean Bruce Poole, *A Guide to Historic Places in Los Angeles County*, 2nd ed. (Dubuque, 1984).

Grim, Tom & Michele, *Away for the Weekend L.A.*, revised ed. (1986).

Hart, James, *A Companion to California*, revised ed. (Berkeley and Los Angeles, 1987).

Hess, Georgia, *Los Angeles and Vicinity: An Annotated Travel Guide* (New York, 1986).

Hoover, Mildred Brooke, *et al.*, *Historic Spots in California*, revised by Douglas E. Kyle (Stanford, 1990).

Kammerton, Roy, *Los Angeles Superlatives* (New York, 1987).

Kanker, Gary and Carol Tarlow, *The California Walking Atlas* (New York, 1990).

Kegan, Stephanie, *Places to Go with Children in Southern California* (San Francisco, 1989).

Kyle, Douglas, *Historic Spots in California*, 4th ed. (1990).

The Junior League of Los Angeles, *Around the Town with Ease: A Guide to L.A. for the Disabled* (Los Angeles, 1984).

Langton, Charan, *Join a Club: Directory of Clubs and Associations of Greater Los Angeles* (Los Angeles, 1983).

Lasker, Toy, *Flashmaps Instant Guide to Los Angeles*, revised ed. (1986).

Lasky, Jane and David Reed, *Crown Insiders' Guide to California* (New York, 1988).

Leaderband, Russ, *A Guidebook to the San Gabriel Mountains of California* (Los Angeles, 1963).

LeBien, Sara, *Museums of Southern California* (Salt Lake, 1988).

Leon, Ruben C., *The Original San Diego Catalogue* (San Diego, 1981).

Los Angeles Mural Conservancy, *Los Angeles Murals: A Guide to 260 Murals at 140 Sites* (Los Angeles, 1990).

Maguire, Molly, editor, *The Raymond Chandler Mystery Map of Los Angeles*, Literary Maps Series (New York, 1986).

Michaelson, Mike, *Weekends Away: L.A.* (New York, 1989).

Moore, Charles W., Peter Becker, and Regula Campbell, *The City Observed: Los Angeles: A Guide to Its Architecture and Landscapes* (New York, 1984).

Mueller, Kimberly J., *California Museum Directory* (Claremont, CA, 1980).

Oberind, Robert, *The Chili Bowls of Los Angeles* (Los Angeles, 1977).

Pearlstone, Zena, *Ethnic L.A.* (Los Angeles, 1990).

Pildas, Ave, *Art Deco in Los Angeles* (New York, 1979).

Pratson, Frederick, *Guide to the Great Attractions of Los Angeles and Beyond* (Chester, CN, 1989).

Rakauskas, Mary, *Los Angeles '91-'92*, Frommer's City Guide Series (New York, 1991). [Note: guide updated biannually]

Reigert, Ray, *Hidden Los Angeles and Southern California* (Berkeley, 1988).

Reisner, Neil, editor, *Jewish Los Angeles: A Guide* (Los Angeles, 1976).

Roberts, George and Jan, *Discover Historic California: A Travel Guide to Over 1500 Places You Can See* (Whittier, 1986).

Robinson, John W., *San Bernardino Mountains* (Berkeley, 1972).

Sanger, Kay and Tom, *Southern California for Kids: One Day Excursions from Los Angeles to San Diego* (New York, 1990).

Schad, Jerry, *Afoot and Afield in Orange County* (Berkeley, 1988).

_____, *Afoot and Afield in San Diego* (Berkeley, 1986).

Schultz, Elizabeth, editor, *Visiting Orange County's Past* (Santa Ana, 1984).

Sigg, Eric, *California Public Gardens, a Visitor's Guide* (Santa Fe, 1991).

Silverman, Jim, editor, *California Kids History Field Trips* (Sonoma, CA, 1990).

Simon, Carey and Charlene Solomon, *Frommer's California with Kids* (New York, 1989).

Silverman, Jim, editor, *California Kids History Field Trips* (Sonoma, CA, 1990).

Spade and Archer, *50 Maps of L.A.* (New York, 1990).

Spencer, J.E., editor, *Day Tours In and Around Los Angeles* (Palo Alto, 1979).

State of California Department of Parks and Recreation, *California Historical Landmarks* (Sacramento, 1975).

Thomas, Bill, *Natural Los Angeles* (New York, 1989).

Thorpe, Edward, *Chandlertown: The Los Angeles of Philip Marlowe* (New York, 1983).

Tuttle, Tom, *Santa Barbara Companion* (San Luis Obispo, 1988).

_____, *Ventura County Companion* (San Luis Obispo, 1988).

Vokac, David, *Destinations of Southern California* (San Diego, 1990).

_____, *Great Tours of California* (San Diego, 1986).

Welch, Ileana, *Historic-Cultural Monuments as Designated by the Cultural Heritage Board, Los Angeles* (Los Angeles, 1980).

Wiley, Stephen, "Los Angeles: 200 Years, 200 Buildings," compiled by Regula Campbell, John Chase, Elizabeth McMillan and John Pastier, *L.A. Architect* 6 (September 1976).

Williamson, Alfred, *Black Olympic Guide to Los Angeles* (Los Angeles, 1984).

Wilson, William, *The Los Angeles Times Book of California Museums* (New York, 1984).

Woolett, William L., "Los Angeles Landmarks," *Historic Preservation* 18 (July/August 1966), pp. 160-163.

Works Progress Administration (WPA), *A Guide to the City of Los Angeles* (New York, 1941).

Wurman, Richard Saul, *L.A./Access* (Los Angeles, 1982).

Yeadon, David, *Exploring Small Towns: 1. Southern California* (Los Angeles, 1973).

APPENDIX B:
HISTORICAL ORGANIZATIONS

Los Angeles County

Acton/Agua Dulce Historical Society
2898 Calmgarden Road
Acton, CA 93510-9637

Alhambra Historical Society
P.O. Box 6687
Alhambra, CA 91802-6687

Altadena Heritage
P.O. Box 218
Altadena, CA 91003

Altadena Historical Society
P.O. Box 144
Altadena, CA 91003-0144

Angelino Heights Community
   Organization
601 E. Edgeware Road
Los Angeles, CA 91733

Arcadia Historical Society
P.O.Box 1804
Arcadia, CA 91077-1804

Archdiocese of Los Angeles
   Archival Center
15151 San Fernando Mission
   Boulevard
Mission Hills, CA 91345

Society of Architectural Historians
4808 Hollywood Boulevard
Los Angeles, CA 90027-5302

Art Deco Society of Los Angeles
P.O. Box 972
Hollywood, CA 90078

Associated Historical Societies
   of Los Angeles County
1298 S. El Molino Avenue
Pasadena, CA 91106

Athletic Foundation Museum
2141 W. Adams Boulevard
Los Angeles, CA 90018

Azusa Historical Society
P.O. Box 1131
Azusa, CA 91702-1131

Friends of the Bailey House
6522 Washington Avenue
Whittier, CA 90601

Baldwin Park Historical Society
P.O. Box 1
Baldwin Park, CA 91706-0001

Friends of Banning Park
41 E. "M" Street
Wilmington, CA 90744

Bel-Air Historical Association
100 Bel-Air Road
Los Angeles, CA 90077

Bellflower Heritage Society
16601 Civic Center Drive
Bellflower, CA 90706-5447

Beverly Hills Historical Society
P.O. Box 1919
Beverly Hills, CA 90213-1919

Burbank Historical Society
1015 W. Olive Avenue
Burbank, CA 91506

Calabasas Historical Society
P.O. Box 8067
Calabasas, CA 91372-8067

California Afro-American Museum
    History & Education Council
600 State Street, Exposition Park
Los Angeles, CA 90037

California Historical Society
1120 Old Mill Road
San Marino, CA 91108

California Society of Theatre
    Historians
2755 Medlow Avenue
Los Angeles, CA 90065

Canoga-Owensmouth Historical
    Society
7248 Owensmouth Avenue
Canoga Park, CA 91303-1529

Carroll Avenue Restoration
    Foundation
1300 Carroll Avenue
Los Angeles, CA 90026

Catalina Island Museum Society
P.O. Box 366
Avalon, CA 90704-0366

Historical Society of Centinela Valley
7634 Midfield Avenue
Los Angeles, CA 90045-3234

Chatsworth Historical Society
10385 Shadow Oak Drive
Chatsworth, CA 91311-2063

Chinese Historical Society
    of Southern California
978 N. Broadway #206
Los Angeles, CA 90012-1729

Chino Historical Society
P.O. Box 972
Chino, CA 91708-0972

Claremont Heritage
P.O. Box 742
Claremont, CA 91711-0742

Covina Valley Historical Society
300 N. Valencia Place
Covina, CA 91723-1824

Cultural Heritage Foundation
225 S. Lake Avenue #1125
Pasadena, CA 91101

Culver City Historical Society
P.O. Box 3428
Culver City, CA 90231-3428

National Society, Daughters of the
    American Revolution
California State Headquarters
201 W. Bennett Avenue
Glendora, CA 91740-2535

Dinsmoor Heritage House
9632 Steele Street
Rosemead, CA 91770-1505

Downey Historical Society
P.O. Box 554
Downey, CA 90241-0554

Drum Barracks Civil War Museum
1052 Banning Boulevard
Wilmington, CA 90744-4604

Duarte Historical Society
P.O. Box 263
Duarte, CA 91010-0263

Eagle Rock Valley Historical Society
2035 Colorado Boulevard
Los Angeles, CA 90041

Electric RY Association
  of Southern California
P.O. Box 24315
Los Angeles, CA 90024-0315

Electric Theater Movie Museum
P.O. Box 1091
Hollywood, CA 90078

El Monte Historical Society
P.O. Box 6307
El Monte, CA 91734-6307

El Pueblo de Los Angeles
  Historic Park
845 N. Alameda Street
Los Angeles, CA 90012-2953

El Pueblo Park Association
845 N. Alameda Street
Los Angeles, CA 90012-2953

El Rancho San Antonio Historical
  Society
6820 Foster Bridge Boulevard
Bell Gardens, CA 90201

El Segundo Public Library
  History Committee
111 W. Mariposa
El Segundo, CA 90245-2299

Encino Historical Society
4862 Zelzah Avenue
Encino, CA 91316

First Century Families
740 Holladay Road
Pasadena, CA 91106

Fort MacArthur Military Museum
  Association
Box 2777, Ft. MacArthur Station
San Pedro, CA 90731-0984

Friends of the Gamble House
4 Westmorland Place
Pasadena, CA 91103-3593

Gene Autry Western Heritage
  Museum
4700 Western Heritage Way
Los Angeles, CA 90027-1462

Gilbert Sproul Museum
12700 Norwalk Boulevard
Norwalk, CA 90650

Glendale Historical Society
P.O. Box 4173
Glendale, CA 91222-0173

Glendora Historical Society
P.O. Box 532
Glendora, CA 91740-0532

Hathaway Ranch Museum
11901 E. Florence Avenue
Santa Fe Springs, CA 90670

Hermosa Beach Historical Society
710 Pier Avenue
Hermosa Beach, CA 90254-3989

Highland Park Heritage Trust
P.O. Box 42894
Los Angeles, CA 90050-0894

Historic Route 66 Association
2127-A Foothill Boulevard #66
La Verne, CA 91750

Hollywood Heritage
P.O. Box 2586
Hollywood, CA 90028-0586

Holmby/Westwood Historical Society
1400 Kelton Avenue #108
Los Angeles, CA 90024-5467

Japanese-American National
  Museum
941 E. 3rd Street
Los Angeles, CA 90099-5296

Jedediah Smith Society
c/o R. Wood, 18052 Rosita Street
Encino, CA 91316

Jewish Historical Society
  of Southern California
6399 Wilshire Boulevard #502
Los Angeles, CA 90048-5708

La Canada-Flintridge Historical
  Society
P.O. Box 541
La Canada, CA 91011-0541

La Mirada Historical Commission
14512 Ialon Road
La Mirada, ca 90638

La Puente Valley Historical Society
P.O. Box 522
La Puente, CA 91747-0522

La Verne Historical Society
1622 Bonita Avenue
La Verne, CA 91750

Las Virgenes Historical Society
P.O. Box 124
Agoura Hills, CA 91376-0124

Leonis Adobe Association
23537 Calabasas Road
Calabasas, CA 91302

Lincoln Heights Preservation
  Association
2652 Workman Street
Los Angeles, CA 90031

Little Landers Historical Society
10110 Commerce Avenue
Tujunga, CA 91042

Lomita Historical Society
P.O. Box 549
Lomita, CA 90717

Historical Society of Long Beach
P.O. Box 1869
Long Beach, CA 90801-1869

Los Angeles City Historical Society
P.O. Box 41046
Los Angeles, CA 90041-0046

Los Angeles Conservancy
727 W. 7th Street #955
Los Angeles, CA 90017

Los Angeles County Fire Department
  Museum Association
1320 N. Eastern Avenue
Los Angeles, CA 90063-3294

Los Angeles County Museum of
  Natural History - History Dept.
900 Exposition Boulevard
Los Angeles, CA 90007

Los Angeles Historic Theatre
  Foundation
P.O. Box 65013
Los Angeles, CA 90065

Los Angeles Maritime Museum
Berth 84 at 6th Street
San Pedro, CA 90731

Los Angeles Police Historical Society
P.O. Box 86105
Los Angeles, CA 90086-0105

Los Angeles State and County
  Arboretum
301 N. Baldwin Avenue
Arcadia, CA 91006

Los Angeles Theatre Organ Society
P.O. Box 1913
Glendale, CA 91209

Los Encinos Historical Society
16756 Moorpark Street
Encino, CA 91436

Los Pobladores 200
5356 Hillmont Avenue
Los Angeles, CA 90041

Manhattan Beach Historical Society
P.O. Box 3355
Manhattan Beach, CA 90266-1355

Monrovia Historical Society
215 E. Lime Avenue
Monrovia, CA 91016

Montebello Historical Society
1600 W. Beverly Boulevard
Montebello, CA 90640-3932

Monterey Park Historical Society
P.O. Box 272
Monterey Park, CA 91754

Mural Conservancy of Los Angeles
P.O. Box 86244
Los Angeles, CA 90086-0244

North Hollywood Historical Society
6026 Ensign Avenue
North Hollywood, CA 91606

Norwalk Historical Heritage
  Commission
P.O. Box 71
Norwalk, CA 90650

Pacific Palisades Historical Society
P.O. Box 1299
Pacific Palisades, CA 90272-1299

Pacific Railroad Historical Society
P.O. Box 80726
San Marino, CA 91118-8726

Pasadena Heritage
80 W. Dayton Street
Pasadena, CA 91105-2002

Pasadena Historical Society
470 W. Walnut Street
Pasadena, CA 91103-3594

Pico Rivera Historical Society
P.O. Box 313
Pico Rivera, CA 90660-0313

Historical Society of Pomona Valley
1569 N. Park Avenue
Pomona, CA 91768-1835

Rancho Los Alamitos Association
6400 E. Bixby Hill Road
Long Beach, CA 90815-4706

Friends of Rancho Los Cerritos
4600 Virginia Road
Long Beach, CA 90807-1916

Rancho de Los Palos Verdes
  Historical Society
P.O. Box 2447
Palos Verdes Peninsula, CA 90274

Rancho Santa Gertrudes Historical
  Society
11901 Florence Avenue
Santa Fe Springs, CA 90670-4498

Redondo Beach Historical Society
P.O. Box 978
Redondo Beach, CA 90277-0270

San Dimas Historical Society
P.O. Box 175
San Dimas, CA 91773-0175

San Fernando Valley Historic Site
  Commission
1303 Glenoaks Boulevard
San Fernando, CA 91340

San Fernando Valley Historical
  Society
10940 Sepulveda Boulevard
Mission Hills, CA 91345-1422

San Gabriel Valley Historical
  Association
546 W. Broadway
San Gabriel, CA 91776

San Marino Historical Society
P.O. Box 80222
San Marino, CA 91118-8222

San Pedro Bay Historical Society
P.O. Box 1568
San Pedro, CA 90733-1568

Santa Clarita Valley Historical
  Society
P.O. Box 875
Newhall, CA 91322

Santa Fe Springs Historical
  Committee
11700 E. Telegraph Road
Santa Fe Springs, CA 90670

Santa Monica Heritage Museum
2612 Main Street
Santa Monica, CA 90405-4002

Santa Monica Historical Society
P.O. Box 3059, Will Rogers Station
Santa Monica, CA 90403-0059

Santa Susanna Mountain Park
  Association
P.O. Box 4831
Chatsworth, CA 91313-4831

Sierra Madre Historical Preservation
  Society
P.O. Box 202
Sierra Madre, CA 91025-0202

The Silent Society
c/o Hollywood Studio Museum
2100 N. Highland Avenue
Hollywood, CA 90068

Historical Society of
  Southern California
200 E. Avenue 43
Los Angeles, CA 90031-1399

South Pasadena Cultural Heritage
1424 Mission Street
South Pasadena, CA 91030

Steamship Historical Society
  Southern California Chapter
351 S. Fuller Avenue #8J
Los Angeles, CA 90036

Swedish American Historical
  Association
California Lutheran University
60 W. Olsen Road
Thousand Oaks, CA 91360-2787

Historical Society of Temple City
P.O. Box 1379
Temple City, CA 91780

Topanga Historical Society
P.O. Box 1214
Topanga, CA 90290-1214

Torrance Historical Society
1345 Post Avenue
Torrance, CA 90501-2621

Venice Historical Society
P.O. Box 2012
Venice, CA 90294-2012

West Adams Heritage Association
2263 S. Harvard Boulevard
Los Angeles, CA 90018

West Antelope Valley Historical
   Society
45026 11th Street West
Lancaster, CA 93534

Westchester Historical Society
c/o M. L. Crockett
7573 S. Sepulveda Boulevard
Westchester, CA 90045

Historical Society of West Covina
P.O. Box 4597
West Covina, CA 91791

Western Hotel Historical Society
P.O. Box 304
Lancaster, CA 93534

Westerners International,
   Huntington Corral
P.O. Box 80241
San Marino, CA 91108-8241

Westerners International,
   Los Angeles Corral
P.O. Box 80250
San Marino, CA 91108-8250

Whittier Historical Society
6755 Newlin Avenue
Whittier, CA 90601-4019

Willmore City Heritage Association
P.O. Box 688
Long Beach, CA 90801

Wilmington Historical Society
P.O. Box 1435
Wilmington, CA 90748-1435

Wilmington Preservation Guild
1217 Lakme Avenue
Wilmington, CA 90744

Windsor Square-Hancock Park
   Historical Society
346 N. Larchmont Boulevard #106
Los Angeles, CA 90004

Workman & Temple Family
   Homestead Museum
15415 Don Julian Road
City of Industry
CA 91745-1029

Kern County

Arvin Historical Society
P.O. Box 96
Arvin, CA 93203

Cowboy Memorial & Library
Star Route, Box 68-A
Caliente, CA 93518

Delano Historical Society
330 Lexington Street
Delano, CA 93215

East Kern Historical Museum
  Society
P.O. Box 2305
California City, CA 93505

Kern-Antelope Historical Society
P.O. Box 325
Rosamond, CA 93560

Kern County Historical Society
P.O. Box 141
Bakersfield, CA 93302

Kern County Museum
3801 Chester Avenue
Bakersfield, CA 93301

Kern River Valley Historical Society
P.O. Box 651
Kernville, CA 93238

Kern Valley Museum
Route 1, Box 200
Lake Isabella, CA 93240

Maturango Museum
  of the Indian Wells Valley
P.O. Box 1776
Ridgecrest, CA 93555

Minter Field Air Museum
Route 11, Box 626
Bakersfield, CA 93312

Shafter Historical Society
P.O. Box 1088
Shafter, CA 93263

Tehachapi Heritage League
P.O. Box 54
Tehachapi, CA 93561

Tehachapi Museum
P.O. Box 54
Tehachapi, CA 93561

Twenty Mule Team Museum
26962 Twenty Mule Team Road
Boron, CA 93516

Wasco Historical Society
P.O. Box 186
Wasco, CA 93280

West Kern Oil Museum
P.O. Box 491
Taft, CA 93268

Orange County

American Aviation Historical Society
2333 Otis
Santa Ana, CA 92704

Anaheim Historical Society
P.O. Box 927
Anaheim, CA 92815

Bowers Museum Association
2002 N. Main Street
Santa Ana, CA 92706

Brea Historical Society
P.O. Box 9764
Brea, CA 92621

Buena Park Historical Society
7842 Whitaker Avenue
Buena Park, CA 90621

Capistrano Indian Council
P.O. Box 304
San Juan Capistrano, CA 92693

Costa Mesa Historical Society
P.O. Box 1764
Costa Mesa, CA 92628

Cypress College Local History
   Association
Cypress College
Cypress, CA 90630

Cypress Heritage Committee
5700 Orange Avenue
Cypress, CA 90630

Dana Point Historical Society
P.O. Box 544
Dana Point, CA 92629

Fountain Valley Historical Society
P.O. Box 8592
Fountain Valley, CA 92728

Friends of Fullerton Arboretum
Heritage House, CSU Fullerton
Fullerton, CA 92634

Fullerton Museum Center
   Association
301 N. Pomona Avenue
Fullerton, CA 92632

Garden Grove Historical Society
12174 Euclid Street
Garden Grove, CA 92640

Governor Pico Mansion Society
14216 Neargrove Road
La Mirada, CA 90638

Heritage Coordinating Council
c/o Fullerton Public Library
353 W. Commonwealth Avenue
Fullerton, CA 92632

Heritage Orange County
515 N. Main Street #208
Santa Ana, CA 92701

The Historical & Cultural
   Foundation of Orange Co.
Jamboree Road, Suite G
Irvine, CA 92714

Huntington Beach Historical Society
19820 Beach Boulevard
Huntington Beach, CA 92648

Irvine Historical Society
5 San Joaquin
Irvine, CA 92715

Laguna Beach Community Historical
Society
P.O. Box 1301
Laguna Beach, CA 92652

Laguna Beach Historical Society
P.O. Box 1526
Laguna Beach, CA 92652

La Habra Old Settlers Historical
Society
600 Linden Lane
La Habra, CA 90631

Leisure World Historical Society
of Laguna Hills
P.O. Box 2220
Laguna Hills, CA 92653

Los Alamitos Museum Association
P.O. Box 15
Los Alamitos, CA 90770

Mother Colony Household
P.O. Box 3246
Anaheim, CA 92803

Newport Beach Historical Society
c/o Sherman Library
614 Dahlia Avenue
Corona Del Mar, CA 92625

Newport Marine Historical Society
2231 Bayside Drive
Corona Del Mar, CA 92625

Old Courthouse Museum Society
211 W. Santa Ana Blvd.
Santa Ana, CA 92701

Orange Community Historical
Society
P.O. Box 5484
Orange, CA 92613-5484

Orange County Archives
1119 E. Chestnut Street
Santa Ana, CA 92701

Orange County Black Historical
Commission
P.O. Box 12542
Santa Ana, CA 92712

Orange County Citrus Historical
Society
18621 Lassen Drive
Santa Ana, CA 92705

Orange County Historical
Commission
P.O. Box 4048
Santa Ana, CA 92702-4048

Orange County Historical Society
P.O. Box 10984
Santa Ana, CA 92711

Orange County Pioneer Council
2320 N. Towner Street
Santa Ana, CA 92706

Orange County Railway Historical
Society
P.O. Box 51
Balboa Island, CA 92662

Pacific Coast Archaeological Society
P.O. Box 10926
Costa Mesa, CA 92627

Pioneer Council of Orange County
2320 N. Towner Street
Orange, CA 92706

Placentia Founders Society
P.O. Box 304
Placentia, CA 92670

Placentia Historical Committee
401 E. Chapman Avenue
Placentia, CA 92670

Saddleback Area Historical Society
P.O. Box 156
El Toro, CA 92630

San Clemente Historical Society
P.O. Box 283
San Clemente, CA 92674-0283

Cultural Arts & Heritage Commission
 City of San Juan Capistrano
32400 Paseo Adelanto
San Juan Capistrano, CA 92675

Friends of Historic San Juan
 Capistrano
P.O. Box 1645
San Juan Capistrano, CA 92693

San Juan Capistrano Historical
 Society
31831 Los Rios Street
San Juan Capistrano, CA 92675

Santa Ana Historical Preservation
 Society
120 Civic Center Drive West
Santa Ana, CA 92701

Santa Ana Mountain Historical
 Society
P.O. Box 322
Silverado, CA 92676

Seal Beach Historical & Cultural
 Society
P.O. Box 152
Seal Beach, CA 90740

Tustin Area Historical Society
P.O. Box 185
Tustin, CA 92681

Westminster Historical Society
P.O. Box 182
Westminster, CA 92683

Yorba Linda Heritage Museum
4802 Olinda Street
Yorba Linda, CA 92686

Riverside County

Coachella Valley Historical Society
P.O. Box 595
Indio, CA 92202

Corona Historic Preservation
  Society
P.O. Box 2904
Corona, CA 91718

Desert Hot Springs Historical
  Society
67-616 E. Desert View
Desert Hot Springs, CA 92240

Hemet Area Museum Association
P.O. Box 2521
Hemet, CA 92343

Malki Museum Association
11-795 Fields Road
Morongo Indian Reservation
Banning, CA 92220

Mission Inn Foundation
3739 6th Street
Riverside, CA 92501

Moreno Valley Historical Society
P.O. Box 66
Moreno Valley, CA 92337

Norco Historical Society
P.O. Box 159
Norco, CA 91760

San Bernardino County

Big Bear Valley Historical Society
P.O. Box 513
Big Bear City, CA 92314

Casa de Rancho Cucamonga Historical Society
P.O. Box 0401
Rancho Cucamonga, CA 91730

City of San Bernardino Historical
   & Pioneer Society
P.O. Box 875
San Bernardino, CA 92402

Fontana Historical Society
P.O. Box 426
Fontana, CA 92334

Inland Empire Museum Foundation
1561 Smiley Heights Drive
Redlands, CA 92373

Mohahve Historical Society
P.O. Box 21
Victorville, CA 92392

Mojave River Valley Museum
   Association
P.O. Box 1282
Barstow, CA 92311

Redlands Area Historical Society
P.O. Box 1024
Redlands, CA 92373

Rialto Historical Society
P.O. Box 413
Rialto, CA 92376

San Bernardino County Museum
   Association
2024 Orange Tree Lane
San Bernardino, CA 92373

San Diego & Imperial Counties

Alpine Historical Society
P.O. Box 382
Alpine, CA 92001

American Aviation Historical Society
5865 Estelle Street
San Diego, CA 92115

Bonita Museum Association
4108 Bonita Road
Bonita, CA 92002

Cabrillo Historical Association
Box 6175
San Diego, CA 92106

Carlsbad Historical Society
P.O. Box 252
Carlsbad, CA 92008

Chinese Historical Society
4408 30th Street
San Diego, CA 92116

Chula Vista Historical Society
P.O. Box 1222
Chula Vista, CA 92012

Civil War Roundtable
P.O. Box 1222
San Diego, CA 92122-0369

Congress of History
of San Diego County
2202 Fairfield Street
San Diego, CA 92110-1108

Coronado Historical Society
P.O. Box 393
Coronado, CA 92118

Del Mar Historical Society
1442 Camino Del Mar
Del Mar, CA 92014

El Cajon Historical Society
P.O. Box 1973
El Cajon, CA 92022

Encinitas Historical Society
949 Eolus Avenue
Leucadia, CA 92024

Escondido Historic Firefighters
Association
310 N. Quince Street
Escondido, CA 92025

Escondido Historical Society
P.O. Box 263
Escondido, CA 92025

Fallbrook Historical Society
P.O. Box 1376
Fallbrook, CA 92028

Fort Guijarros Museum Foundation
P.O. Box 231500
San Diego, CA 92123

Hemet Area Museum Association
440 N. Taylor
Hemet, CA 92343

Historical Shrine Foundation
2482 San Diego Avenue
San Diego, CA 92110

Imperial Valley Pioneers Historical
Society
P.O. Box 224
Imperial. CA 92251

Julian Historical Society
P.O. Box 513
Julian, CA 92036

La Jolla Historical Society
P.O. Box 2085
La Jolla, CA 92037

Lakeside Historical Society
P.O. Box 1423
Lakeside, CA 92040

La Mesa Historical Society
P.O. Box 882
La Mesa, CA 92041

Lemon Grove Historical Society
P.O. Box 624
Lemon Grove, CA 92045

MCRD Museum Historical Society
P.O. Box 33015
San Diego, CA 92103

Maritime Museum Association
  of San Diego
1306 N. Harbor Drive
San Diego, CA 92101

Mountain Empire Historical Society
P.O. Box 394
Campo, CA 92006

National City Historical Society
P.O. Box 1251
National City, CA 92050

North Park Historical Society
3815 Utah Street
San Diego, CA 92104

Pacific Beach Historical Society
P.O. Box 9200
San Diego, CA 92109

Potrero East County Museum
  Society
P.O. Box 104
Potrero, CA 90263

Poway Historical Society
P.O. Box 19
Poway, CA 92064

Ramona Pioneer Historical Society
P.O. Box 625
Ramona, CA 92065

Rancho Santa Fe Historical Society
P.O. Box 2414
Rancho Santa Fe, CA 92067

San Clemente Historical Society
P.O. Box 283
San Clemente, CA 92672

San Diego Electric RY
  Association
P.O. Box 89068
San Diego, CA 92138

San Diego Historical Society
P.O. Box 81825
San Diego, CA 92138

San Diego Jewish Historical Society
3942 Liggett Drive
San Diego, CA 92106

San Diego Military Heritage Society
P.O. Box 33672
San Diego, CA 92103

San Marcos Historical Society
105 Richmar Avenue
San Marcos, CA 92069

San Pasqual Battlefield Association
15808 San Pasqual Valley Road
Escondido, CA 92025

Santee Historical Society
10765 Woodside Road
Santee, CA 92071-3198

SOHO (Save Our Heritage
    Organization)
P.O. Box 3571
San Diego, CA 92103

Spring Valley Historical Society
9050 Memory Lane
Spring Valley, CA 92077

Temecula Historical Society
P.O. Box 264
Temecula, CA 92390

Vista Ranchos Historical Society
P.O. Box 1032
Vista, CA 92063

Westerners International,
    San Diego Corral
P.O. Box 7174
San Diego, CA 92107

Santa Barbara County

Carpinteria Valley Historical Society
Box 103
Carpinteria, CA 93013

El Presidio de Santa Barbara
   State Historic Park
123 E. Canon Perdido
Santa Barbara, CA 93101

Goleta Valley Historical Society
304 N. Los Carneros Road
Goleta, CA 93117

Lompoc Valley Historical Society
P.O. Box 88
Lompoc, CA 93438

Mission La Purisima Concepcion
   State Historic Park
Purisima Road
Lompoc, CA 93438

Old Mission Santa Ynez
1760 Mission Drive
Solvang, CA 93463

Santa Barbara Historical Society
P.O. Box 578
Santa Barbara, CA 93102

Santa Barbara Mission
Archive/Library
2201 Laguna Street
Santa Barbara, CA 93105

Santa Barbara Trust for Historic
   Preservation
P.O. Box 388
Santa Barbara, CA 93102

Santa Maria Valley Historical Society
P.O. Box 584
Santa Maria, CA 93454

Santa Ynez Valley Historical
   Society
P.O. Box 181
Santa Ynez, CA 93460

Ventura County

Albinger Archaeological Museum
113 E. Main Street
Ventura, CA 93001

California Oil Museum/Unocal
1003 Main Street
Santa Paula, CA 93060

Conejo Valley Historical Society
P.O. Box 1025
Thousand Oaks, CA 91358

Fillmore Historical Society
P.O. Box 314
Fillmore, CA 93015

Mission San Buenaventura
211 E. Main Street
Ventura, CA 93001

Moorpark Historical Society
P.O. Box 662
Moorpark, CA 93021

Ojai Valley Historical Society
P.O. Box 204
Ojai, CA 93023

Pleasant Valley Historical Society
P.O. Box 570
Camarillo, CA 93011

Santa Paula Historical Society
118 S. 8th Street
Santa Paula, CA 93060

CEC SeaBee Museum
Code 22-M, Building 99
Navy Constuction Battalion Center
Port Hueneme, CA 93043

Simi Valley Historical Society
P.O. Box 351
Simi Valley, CA 93062

Stagecoach Inn Museum
51 S. Ventu Park Road
Newbury Park, CA 91320

Strathern Historical Park
137 Strathern Place
Simi Valley, CA 93062

Swedish-American Historical
   Society
c/o California Lutheran University
60 W. Olsen Road
Thousand Oaks, CA 91360

Ventura County Museum
   of History & Art
100 E. Main Street
Ventura, CA 93001

GEOGRAPHICAL INDEX

(Listed by Outing numbers)

Cherry Valley Riverside County 87.
China Lake 247.
Chino Los Angeles County 55, 153, 187, 195, 200, 211, 332, 349.
Chiriaco Summit Riverside County 330.
Claremont Los Angeles County 53, 58, 218, 220, 304.
Compton Los Angeles County 284.
Corona Riverside County 258.
Corona del Mar Orange County 142, 351.
Coronado San Diego County 94.
Costa Mesa Orange County 75, 141, 183.
Covina Los Angeles County 57, 224.
Cucamonga (see Rancho Cucamonga)
Culver City Los Angeles County 28.

Dana Point Orange County 265, 342.
Desert Hot Springs Riverside County 278.
Dominguez Los Angeles County 127, 343.
Downey Los Angeles County 72, 286, 313.
Duarte Los Angeles County 50, 53.

Eagle Rock (Los Angeles) Los Angeles County 16, 299.
El Centro Imperial County 99.
El Monte Los Angeles County 57, 149, 262, 332, 349.
El Segundo Los Angeles County 205.
El Sereno Los Angeles County 5.
El Toro Orange County 81, 321, 350.
Encinitas San Diego County 93.
Encino Los Angeles County 39.
Escondido San Diego County 89, 91.

Fallbrook San Diego County 90.
Fillmore Ventura County 107.
Fontana San Bernardino County 53.
Fort Tejon State Historic Park Kern County 267.
Fountain Valley Orange County 77.
Fullerton Orange County 79, 80, 350.

Garden Grove Orange County 78.
Gardena Los Angeles County 186, 226.
Glendale Los Angeles County 16, 17, 128, 241, 307, 343.
Glendora Los Angeles County 51, 53, 114, 224.
Goleta Santa Barbara County 101, 322, 253.

Malibu   Los Angeles County   118, 121, 177, 249, 345.
Manhattan Beach   Los Angeles County   66, 142, 151.
Marina del Rey   Los Angeles County   242.
Mission Hills   Los Angeles County   39, 119, 204, 236, 257, 343.
Monrovia   Los Angeles County   49, 51, 53, 317.
Montebello   Los Angeles County   169.
Monterey Park   Los Angeles County   169, 297.
Moreno Valley   Riverside County   332.

Needles   San Bernardino County   53.
Newberry Park   Ventura County   108.
Newhall (see Santa Clarita)
Newport Beach   Orange County   141, 142, 342.
Niland   Imperial County   99.
Norco   Riverside County   83.
North Hollywood   Los Angeles County   179.
Northridge   Los Angeles County   236.
Norwalk   Los Angeles/Orange Counties   70, 77.

Oak Glen   San Bernardino County   87.
Oceanside   San Diego County   92, 352.
Ojai   Ventura County   111, 212, 354.
Ontario   San Bernardino County   114, 153, 348.
Orange   Orange County   78.
Oxnard   Ventura County   122, 287, 342.

Pacific Palisades   Los Angeles County   62, 126, 177.
Pala   San Diego County   90, 251.
Palm Springs   Riverside County   86.
Palos Verdes   Los Angeles County   65, 341.
Pasadena   Los Angeles County   43, 45-48, 120, 128, 150, 165, 189, 210, 217, 221, 233, 241, 281, 298, 300, 301, 306, 311,333, 344.
Perris   Riverside County   283.
Piru   Ventura County   107.
Placentia   Orange County   78, 79.
Pomona   Los Angeles County   53, 54, 83, 114, 154, 211, 257, 262, 348.
Port Hueneme   Ventura County   109.

Rancho Cucamonga   San Bernardino County   53, 54, 56, 262, 348.
Rancho Santa Fe   San Diego County   93.
Randsburg   Kern County   279.

Red Mountain   San Bernardino County   279.
Redlands   San Bernardino County   56, 84, 308, 349.
Redondo Beach   Los Angeles County   66, 142, 151, 246.
Rialto   San Bernardino County   53.
Ridgecrest   San Bernardino County   247.
Riverside   Riverside County   83, 84, 154.
Rosemead   Los Angeles County   57.

San Bernardino   San Bernardino County   53.
San Clemente   Orange County   142.
San Diego   San Diego County   94-98, 132, 142, 215, 244,
   291, 342, 352.
San Dimas   Los Angeles County   53, 114, 269.
San Fernando   Los Angeles County   39.
San Gabriel   Los Angeles County   119, 325.
San Juan Capistrano   Orange County
San Marino   Los Angeles County   44, 45, 124, 133, 223,
   227, 232, 325, 347.
San Pasqual Battlefield State Park   San Diego County
89.
San Pedro   Los Angeles County   65, 162, 199, 320, 337,
   340, 342.
Santa Ana   Orange County   74, 208.
Santa Barbara   Santa Barbara County   101-103, 142, 148,
   248, 287, 353.
Santa Clarita   Los Angeles County   41, 329.
Santa Fe Springs   Los Angeles County   71.
Santa Monica   Los Angeles County   121, 140, 142, 177,
   202, 214, 225, 285, 324.
Santa Paula   Ventura County   107, 328.
Santa Ynez   Santa Barbara County   104.
Seal Beach   Orange County   75, 142.
Sierra Madre   Los Angeles County   50, 124.
Simi Valley   Ventura County   107, 144.
Solvang   Santa Barbara County   106.
South Pasadena   Los Angeles County   43.
Sugarloaf   San Bernardino County   85.
Sun Valley   Los Angeles County   220.
Sylmar   Los Angeles County   37.

Taft   Kern County   161.
Tarzana   Los Angeles County   214.
Temecula   Riverside County   89, 251.
Thousand Oaks   Ventura County   181, 338.
Torrance   Los Angeles County   188, 199, 337.

Tujunga   Los Angeles County   36, 235.
Tustin   Orange County   77.
Twentynine Palms   San Bernardino County   277

Upland   San Bernardino County   53.

Van Nuys   Los Angeles County   35, 329.
Vandenberg Air Force Base   Santa Barbara County   288.
Venice   Los Angeles County   67, 229.
Ventura   Ventura County   108, 110, 112, 212, 342.
Victorville   San Bernardino County   32, 53.
Vista   San Diego County   91.

Walnut   Los Angeles County   54.
Westchester (Los Angeles)   Los Angeles County   60, 257, 340, 343.
West Covina   Los Angeles County   186.
Westminster   Orange County   75, 340.
Westwood   Los Angeles County   62.
Whittier   Los Angeles County   69, 271.
Wilmington   Los Angeles County   205, 270, 280, 340, 344.
Woodland Hills   Los Angeles County   264.

Yorba Linda   Orange County   79, 197.
Yucaipa   San Bernardino County   87.
Yucca Valley   Riverside County   276.

TOPICAL INDEX

(Listed by Outing numbers)

East Indian history & culture   177.
Electric railway   3, 75, 80, 281, 283.

Filipino history & culture   334.
Finnish history & culture   165.
French history & culture   163, 316, 324.

Gardens & parks   7, 17, 33, 42, 46, 53, 59, 68, 71, 86, 88,
   93, 103, 220-223, 241, 329, 341, 346, 347, 351.
Geology   16, 52, 85, 216, 217, 218, 219.
German history & culture   93, 337.
Greek history & culture   199.

Horticulture   40, 44, 47, 50, 53, 220, 221, 222, 252, 299.
Hungarian history & culture   170.

Indians (see Native Americans, or East Indian)
Irish history & culture   34, 185.
Italian history & culture   1, 153, 163, 176, 198.

Japanese history & culture   20, 77, 164, 176, 178, 180, 186,
   189, 192, 222, 223, 329.
Jewish history & culture   19, 166, 167, 318.

Korean history & culture   193.

Landscape & the environment   7, 38, 42, 52, 53, 61, 85,
   104, 216-224, 248, 249, 259, 273, 281, 315.
Literature & books   5, 10, 12, 17, 28, 107, 112, 156, 204,
   206, 214, 225-235.

Mexican-American history & culture   1, 97, 100, 139, 163,
   169, 237, 316, 325, 343, 353.
Military   75, 83, 89, 102, 109, 267, 268, 288, 289, 320, 321,
   330, 331, 332.
Mining   41, 85, 90, 259, 261, 276, 277, 279.
Missions   39, 82, 90, 92, 98, 102, 105, 106, 119, 204, 251.
Motion pictures   18-33, 41, 61, 152, 202, 219, 239, 243, 260,
   264.
Murals   35, 46, 103, 137, 139, 140, 169, 175, 201, 2038
Music & dance   8, 22, 37, 58, 236-242, 245, 246, 252, 298,
   302, 313, 319.

Native American history & culture   88, 90, 105, 111, 236,
   247-255, 288.

Native plants   7, 90, 103, 105, 220, 221, 252.

Oil   41, 107, 161.

Parades   99, 100, 101, 106, 109, 186, 193, 275, 276, 306,
    314, 326, 333, 339, 340, 342.
Photography & photographic equipment   24, 39, 84, 86.
Polish history & culture   197.
Polynesian history & culture   184, 190.
Portuguese history & culture   162.

Railroads & trains   7, 41, 58, 80, 88, 96, 107, 110. 121, 148,
    152, 280, 283, 322.
Ranch life   38, 40, 41, 55, 70, 257, 263, 274, 277.
Russian history & culture   335, 355.

Samoan history & culture   184, 194
Schools (see also, Colleges & universities)   5, 58, 79, 81, 87,
    104, 124, 132, 153, 205, 218.
Scottish history & culture   183, 200, 307.
Sculpture   17, 41, 53, 134, 138, 141, 142, 215, 264.
Ships   64, 65, 68, 98, 109, 110, 112, 113, 162, 265, 320, 327,
    339, 340, 342.
Space science   45, 286, 288, 291, 292.
Sports (see Athletics)
Stagecoaches & stage stops (see also, Wagons) 53, 103, 104,
    256, 258, 262, 280, 290.
Swedish history & culture   181, 196, 338.
Swiss history & culture   182.

Television   25, 26, 29.
Thai history & culture   179.
Toys   202, 205, 207, 208.

Victorian architecture   6, 8, 13, 54, 70, 71, 73, 74, 76, 77,
    79, 84, 94, 103, 107, 310, 314, 347-349.

Wagons & carriages   53, 97, 99, 103, 104, 108, 155, 255,
    256, 258, 262, 272, 273, 280, 290.
Water supply   159, 160, 329, 330.
Wineries   53, 55, 89, 104, 153, 176.
Women's history   10, 11, 22, 35, 37, 51, 65, 74, 107, 121,
    122, 131, 132, 138, 144, 154, 175, 232, 236, 293-305.

Yugoslavian history and culture   172.